HOW TO LIVE THE DREAM:

THINGS EVERY VAN LIFER NEEDS TO KNOW

Kristine Hudson

ISBN: 978-1-953714-16-9

Download The Audio Version Of This Book For Free!

If you love listening to audiobooks on-the-go or enjoy the narration as you read along, I have great news for you. You can download the audio book version of

HOW TO LIVE THE DREAM:

THINGS EVERY VAN LIFER NEEDS TO KNOW

Kristine Hudson

for FREE just by signing up for a FREE 30-day audible trial.

For Audible UK:

https://tinyurl.com/y9g5px72

For Audible US:

https://tinyurl.com/ya6f3rmd

Reviews

Reviews and feedback help improve this book and the author. If you enjoy this book, we would greatly appreciate it if you could take a few moments to share your opinion and post a review on Amazon.

Contents

Section 1: Making the Big Decision

There's a certain romance to the idea of living on the road. Traveling wherever the wind blows. Leaving nothing except footprints. Taking nothing but pictures.

The media is awash with images of attractive, wind-swept people, staring out of their windows at an awe-inspiring vista. Mountains, oceans, and fields so far and wide, you can hardly see the horizon. All these images make van living look like an incredible option. Not only do you get to shed the boring, stale, workaday lifestyle, but you get to wake up wherever you want.

To many, van living is the ultimate goal. It is the dream that just won't go away. While there's tons of material in the media explaining how amazing van life is, there is little to help you prepare for the reality of life on the road.

We'll explore what it takes to hack a nomadic lifestyle in the 21st century, with road tips provided from actual American van dwellers. Throughout this book, you'll find "Advice from the Road," which contains tips, tricks, and details provided by folks who have personally practiced the van lifestyle.

We'll start with all the considerations you'll need to keep in mind before making the decision to follow your wanderlust. We'll also go through the process of choosing your new home, as well as things to consider when creating and utilizing space. Budgeting, as well as managing income and expenditures, is also a huge part of van life. We'll help you get packed and ready to hit the trails, with some tips and tricks for staying happy and learning to find your home on the road.

You might be surprised at how involved the process is, but bear in mind that this is always your adventure. You can ramp up or tame the journey to meet your preferred lifestyle. After all, this is *your* life's dream!

Chapter 1: Why Do I Want to Live in a Van?

Before you start the engine and bid farewell to your friends and family — before you even have an engine to start — you must get in touch with your dream. This may sound a bit New Age, but the reality is that you are about to commit to a very significant lifestyle change by living in a van. Whether you have a regular nine-to-five job that you're sick of, or have been a freewheeling freelancer for years, van living is nothing like what you have experienced to date.

You will not be able to come home. If you have a rough day, you won't be able to "just stay in and order a pizza." The routines that have come to rule your life will no longer exist.

If hearing that makes your heart beat a little faster, you're not alone. The primary reason people choose van life is because they are sick of having a home and a yard, or an apartment and neighbors. They're tired of commuting to work. They don't want to spend an entire weekend cleaning floors and dusting knick-knacks. They want to live.

If you identify with this, you're on the right track. But here's one important question to ask yourself: By living on the road, what do you hope to achieve? What deep, burning need in your life will van living satisfy, and are you prepared to make a significant number of sacrifices to find that lifestyle?

Let us point out before you start feeling less certain about van living: there are different types of van living experiences.

First, there's the type of Van Lifers who maintain their home and daily lifestyle but use their van as a mobile escape. In previous decades, truly adventurous families had vacation properties, such as beach condos or lakeside cabins. The modern twist on this is to make the holiday home a van, so adventure may take place anywhere you can imagine to drive.

Then there are the semi-permanent nomads. These folks may have a PO Box in a permanent location. They may live full time in the van, but they stay tied to a particular area, whether that be an RV park, long-term campground, or the general vicinity. They may take off for an adventure now and again, but they migrate only around a certain radius.

Lastly, there are the true devotees. These folks plan to see as much as possible and do as much as they can before their time on this planet expires. They hope to never see the same sunset or sunrise — though if they do, they maintain it's purely because they wanted to see that view one more time. These folks don't plan to land on terra firma any time soon and are fully prepared to have all their needs fulfilled by life on the road.

You may fit firmly within one of these categories. You might find yourself somewhere in shades in between. Remember, there is no "wrong way" to organize your dreams. The goal of van life is to fulfill a need you have deep in your soul, and if your soul decides it wants to come home and do a load of laundry, that does not mean you're not accomplishing your dream.

When it comes to van living, there are a few aspects of the lifestyle that tend to be magnets to most people considering the option. Let's explore those in more detail.

The Chance to Live Off-Grid
While "keeping up with the Joneses'" has been part of the American Dream for over a century, there are many who are no longer impressed with this ideal. A larger house might be a great fantasy, but that involves a heftier house payment — which means working more hours. And a bigger house means more "stuff," like furniture and decorations. Owning more means increased upkeep, higher utility bills, taking care of a bigger lawn, etc. For some folks, this sounds less like the American Dream and more like a terrifying nightmare.

A van does not have a mortgage, though you might find yourself making payments on your roaming home — we'll discuss that more later. A van doesn't have utility bills. A van doesn't have an attic to maintain or a basement that floods when it rains. A van doesn't have noisy neighbors. You will do no yard work.

But that doesn't mean it's completely carefree. A van is a mechanical invention, and it can break down. Windows can crack. Tires can blow. You'll need to find new ways of creating power. You will not have running water unless you create that option. If anything breaks, you will have to take care of it, and immediately. While van living does mean you'll be living off the grid, it does not mean you'll live without responsibility.

The Ability to Be Self-Sustaining

Urban and suburban lifestyles require constant connection. You have neighbors. You have coworkers. You have friends. Your social obligations require you to continually connect with these individuals in order to sustain your network and relationships. How much time do you have to yourself?

Traveling the country solo, with just the wind as your copilot may seem like the best way to completely disconnect and shed all these social responsibilities. You have the chance to be alone with your own mind and learn who you are. You can discover how your mind and soul work, and uncover the mystery of who you want to become before your time on this planet draws to a close.

When you work 40-80 hours a week, 52 weeks of the year, you lose the connection with yourself and become the routine that maintains your lifestyle. Being on the road will tear you away from what you've known as life, and guide you to understanding who you really are.

And that means completely upending that routine. What will you do on Saturday mornings, if not going to meet friends for brunch, followed by cleaning the bathroom? When Monday morning arrives, how will you greet the day if you don't have to shower and get ready for work before the sun rises?

For many of us, our lifestyle is determined by what we need to do to keep doing the same thing. When you live on the road, you no longer have to sustain these patterns. While you certainly can continue to work in an office if that's your preference, you won't feel the pressure to work 12-hour days to pay the bills. It certainly won't take you multiple hours to clean the bathroom. Every aspect of your life will be simplified to the most basic needs, rather than creating a level of comfort.

Will you be able to live without guidelines, restrictions, or limitations of someone else? Will you choose instead to learn how to self-sustain, the way humans were intended to live?

The Freedom to Roam
When you no longer live under the demands of someone else's schedule, you have the ability to create your own agenda. This means you can go anywhere you want. You can see what you want to see. Do what you want to do. You don't have to be in the boardroom for a meeting at 3 pm every day. You don't have to take a day off work to wait for the repair technician because the cable isn't working. You have the freedom to dictate your own schedule, and your home has four rubber wheels that are designed to take you anywhere.

This may sound absolutely ideal for many, but it can also cause a bit of anxiety for others. Choice paralysis is real, and some people might have a hard time deciding what to do next. After all, hunting and gathering is no longer a truly viable option in the United States, so following the herds and water sources is not a requirement for survival.

The freedom to roam also means you have to decide where you're going to go. You may be the type of person who has to know where you're going to be on any given day, and that's a hard habit to break. When it is midnight and you're driving through a severe thunderstorm, you might regret not having found a place to park and turn in for the night. After all, though you may shed the responsibilities of suburban life, you'll never get past biological needs!

Even at its most liberating, van life still demands a certain amount of planning and research. While you'll have the ability to go anywhere you want, you still have to acknowledge the practicalities, legalities, and realities that await you.

See the World on Your Own Time

Now that you are no longer living under someone else's agenda, you have to create your own. This doesn't have to be a hard-set "to-do" list of daily chores, but instead, a list of goals and accomplishments you'd like to have under your belt in time.

Before you hit the road, create a list of places you'd like to see, or things you'd like to do. Want to summit El Capitan? Fantastic. Have a burning desire to see the sun rise on the southernmost point of the country? Excellent. Consider themes and key points of interest that really get your blood pumping. Now that you have this freedom, it's time to make the most of it.

Once you are on the road, you truly have the ability to see the world. If you choose to make van living a full-time lifestyle, then this is not a vacation. You do not have to be back in the office in three days' time. You don't need to hire someone to water the plants. If you are going to be a part-time road warrior, however, then you will need to adjust accordingly, which makes having an agenda even more important. After all, the reason you've chosen to live in a van, instead of a tiny house or exotic cave, is because you embrace mobility.

Consider the Alternative

Now that you've really defined why you feel compelled to live in a van, consider the option of not living in a van.

That's right — the time has come to ask yourself why this is so important. One way to make your desires truly transparent is to look at the situation from the flip side.

What if you don't pursue this? What if you just stay home, continue working your job, making sure your knick-knacks don't get dusty? Maybe you go camping every weekend to scratch that wanderlust itch, but you don't go all the way into van living. Would this be something that you would regret?

Living in a van is demanding. Physically, you'll find you have to spend a significant amount of time driving. Your gym routine is likely a thing of the past, too, and you'll have to find ways to feed yourself that don't involve a full-sized kitchen. Emotionally, you will be alone with your thoughts, all day, every day. Are you prepared to keep yourself entertained? Are you comfortable addressing all of the thoughts, hopes, dreams, and emotions that have been ignored while you go with the urban flow? Mentally, you're going to have to prepare for a new set of dangers and challenges. While remaining open to rewards that would never be possible when living in a two bedroom walk-up.

Successful van life is more than just knowing how to set up your bathroom and innovative storage. It is far more than dangling tan legs out the window or watching the sun rise and set in new, amazing places. This is an opportunity to shed not only your electric bill, but every expectation that has ever been made of you and your abilities. You will need to learn a new set of survival skills, and the things that made you feel "comfortable" in a home-dwelling lifestyle will no longer be the same.

In many ways, van living is an entirely new life, and this is a journey that will require dedication and preparation in order to serve you well. You will learn much along the way; in fact, many would argue that you'll learn far more about life when living on the road. However, you have to be prepared to execute those skills and to be ready for a new set of challenges.

Chapter 2: The Reality of Van Living - Doing Your Homework

Before making the decision to commit to van life, it is important that you understand all the challenges and potential hazards that come with the lifestyle. While you have a new and exciting level of freedom, you are going to encounter a new level of responsibility. Not only do you have complete control over where you roam, but you are required to solve every problem that might arise.

This is not to say these problems are too hard to solve. In fact, being prepared before you hit the road will help turn these problems into a variety of inconveniences, rather than taking all the zest out of van living. You will find that one of the key elements to a successful van lifestyle is planning and preparation, which can begin as soon as you start day-dreaming about the possibilities.

Let's look at some of the key areas in which you'll need to practice good planning and preparation. This includes: knowing how to keep up with van maintenance, being aware of your equipment, keeping it in good working order, and finding places to park and catch up on rest.

Van Maintenance
Taking care of yourself will be critical on the road, but taking care of your van will be equally important. Therefore, you will need to learn some basic van maintenance.

There are many aspects of vehicle repair and preservation that are relatively simple and can be conducted on nearly any flat service. Being able to check, monitor, and replenish your fluids is a great place to start. Oil, coolant, transmission fluid, brake fluid, and power steering fluid are all things that will need constant observation when you live on the road. They need very little automotive skill to learn where to find the input point, what type to buy, and when to top off your supply.

You may want to invest a little more effort into your overall maintenance skills in order to preserve your overall autonomy. There are two basic facts that apply to any van living situation:
1. A vehicle in motion will require more maintenance, more frequently.
2. Vans require specialized mechanics in many cases. Some vans have a different type of mechanical engineering, and others are

too heavy for a regular repair shop's lift system. In either case, you will not be able to simply roll your van up to any mechanic's shop for basic maintenance.

These two reasons make a compelling case for learning how to do your own basic vehicle care, such as changing oil and oil filters, as well as air filters and fuel filters. While finding a mechanic who can work on your van might be tricky, finding an auto parts store that carries the items you need is far less challenging.

Knowing your vehicle inside and out isn't entirely necessary, especially if you have a particular mechanical ineptitude; however, you will want to become familiar enough with your van to diagnose certain issues. You may want to consider a few automotive classes or online courses. You can also enhance your knowledge or learning process by checking out online videos, which you can bookmark for future reference.

Once you have learned the basic mechanical anatomy and processes of your vehicle, you will want to keep several references in your vehicle at all times. The first is the owner's manual. It can be somewhat tricky to track down owner's manuals, especially if you are purchasing an older vehicle or one that has already gone through several rounds of remodels or rehabs. However, you should be able to find supplemental information online that can provide key information on motors, as well as years, makes, and models of a variety of vehicles.

In addition to the owner's manual, you will want a repair handbook specific to your vehicle type. Understanding the basics in your vehicle could save you hundreds of dollars and days of possible lost time, simply by being able to identify where the problem is.

Lastly, you will need to keep immaculate maintenance records of your own. Not only will this help you track when you need regular preventive care, like oil changes and tire rotations, but can help you record any patterns or trouble areas, such as brakes wearing down too quickly or hoses needing replacing more frequently than you imagined.

As you learn about your vehicle, pay attention to what tools you'll need to fix common repair techniques. Often these tools will be useful for a variety of maintenance in and around the van and will become part of your onboard kit.

Your Key Equipment

While we'll discuss the type of equipment you'll need in your van further in Section 2 and 3, it is important to note that you will also be responsible for the care and maintenance of the equipment within your van.

This can include everything from your cooking surface to your water and power systems, to your most low-tech equipment, such as a cooler or tent.

When living in a van, you do not have the luxury of packing loads of supplies. Instead, you have limited space and thus need to pack only necessary gear, and tools essential for the repair of that gear. For example, instead of packing a main tent and a spare, a better use of space is to pack a tent and a tent repair kit.

You may also be limited as to what you can easily replace. Buying new screens for your windows may seem tempting, but your budget will dictate whether you can do this. Instead, consider learning how to repair the equipment that you will have onboard.

This will likely mean investing in tools and common repair elements, such as tarps, duct tape, twine, and more. As you learn how each piece of equipment in your van works, learn how it can fail to function and what you'll need to have onboard to keep it in good working order. Again, this will save you hundreds of dollars and tons of frustration.

Locations for Landing

At some point in your day, you will need to rest. Your van will also likely thank you for the break. Therefore, you will need to know where, when, and how long you can park your van in a variety of locations. After all, getting a ticket or threatened with towing will put a real damper on your experience... and budget.

Unfortunately, "free parking" is more a thing of the past in inhabited areas. Loiterers and an influx of illegal activity have really put a damper on being able to park and sleep for the night. However, there are some locations in which you'll be able to catch at least a few hours of shut-eye.

Some retail locations — especially stores that supply outdoor activities — still permit adventurers of all kinds a few hours to rest in their parking lots. Before you make assumptions, however, be sure to check with store management to understand the parameters of their offerings. Also, you'll always want to obey posted signage. Sometimes the business does not own the parking lot, so separate rules will apply to those traveling through.

Truck stops and rest areas are other popular spots for a quick rest. Again, there may be time limits on your stay. Always obey posted signs and local ordinances. These will generally be posted in a common area of the rest stop.

Another fantastic resource for free parking is National Land. This refers to land within National Forests or territory that is not otherwise owned or maintained by a private owner. The majority of this land lies west of the Mississippi River, and can be a fantastic opportunity for van people. While these are not paved or maintained sites, and they will not feature luxuries such as even the most remote vault toilet, you can find flat, remote places where you can legally park for free. Once again, there may be limits on how long you can stay in these spots.

Finding spots to park may seem like a game of roulette, but there are actually many resources available to help you hunt down options. (These have been included in the **Resource Guide** at the end of the book.) Van people are, above all, sympathetic to each others' quests and willing to help out whenever possible. Therefore, a wealth of information can be found on-line or even by talking to others on the road.

Van living does require knowledge and skills, beyond that which you may have at the outset of planning your new lifestyle. However, keep in mind that any lifestyle has a learning curve. When you moved into your house, for example, you probably had to learn where all the light switches were, or how to get the hot water to work. Van living is a very similar experience — you need to learn a new skill set. But once learned, it will help you immeasurably and become part of your daily rituals.

Chapter 3: The Human Element of Van Life- Health and Wealth

Besides requiring a certain amount of mechanical know-how, there are quite a few existential challenges you will encounter on the road, which re-quire mental preparation before you embark on your new mobile lifestyle.

One thing to keep in mind is that you are by and large in control of your overall experience. Everything you have, you make happen. You will no longer have the opportunity to walk over to the neighbor's house to borrow a cup of sugar. You will need to be prepared for everything the road throws at you.

At the same time, do not be bogged down by responsibility. While van living is a totally different type of lifestyle, in time, it will become second nature. Just as you had to figure out life in your first apartment or how to adapt to your first job; you will learn to live in a van. However, be gentle with yourself and allow yourself time to get comfortable with the notion. In the early days, you may question your decision or find yourself unsure of what to do next. This is normal. We all experience growing pains and a learning curve whenever we make huge changes in our lives.

To begin, you can prepare for your new lifestyle before you even purchase your van. Not only can you learn maintenance procedures and parking regulations, but you can prepare yourself for the challenges you'll face as a human as well.

Your Health

In addition to taking care of your van and equipment, you will need to take care of yourself while you are on the road. Not only will your body need to be fed when it is hungry, have access to adequate clean water, and rest when necessary, but you will need regular maintenance as well. Staying in perfect health becomes more complicated when you are on the road. You will be exposed to a new world of germs, and you won't be able to visit your regular doctor if you start feeling under the weather.

There are many things you can do, to ensure your health is always a priority:

1. Pack a first aid kit, including care for multiple types of wounds and injuries. This includes bandages, wraps, antiseptic cream, absorbent pads, athletic wrap and tape, as well as instant ice packs and heat packs.
2. Pack a wellness kit, too. This can include cold medicine, over-the-counter products for pain and fever, topical cream for sprains and strains, throat lozenges, sleep aids, and products for heart-burn or upset stomachs.
3. Consider a daily vitamin. Even with a refrigeration system, you won't be able to have full, immediate access to all the fresh fruit and vegetables you had at home, so make sure your body and immune system are fully prepared.
4. If you are on any daily prescriptions, talk to your prescribing physician before you hit the road. You may wish to transfer your prescriptions to a national pharmacy chain and purchase prescriptions in 90-day supplies whenever possible. Often, this will require your doctor's approval. Also share with your doctor where you will be traveling, as some states do not permit non-residents to pick up certain prescriptions. You do not want

to suffer the side effects of missed essential medication while on the road, as that can quickly become serious. Planning ahead with your doctor will ensure you are ahead of the game.

5. Illness will happen. Before you hit the road, consider what your backup plan will be in case you are too sick to drive for several days. Hotels and long-term parking facilities can be expensive but may prove necessary when you are sick. The alternative of driving while you are unable has far greater consequences.

6. Consider your insurance situation, as well. What will happen if you need to go to the hospital, emergency room, or urgent care? In the United States, private insurance is often a requirement to offset very high expenses. What is your plan for carrying insurance during your travels?

Mental Wellness

In addition to your physical well-being, consider your mental health, as well. Being on the road is not always fun! The road will bring more rewards than regrets, but there will be days when you are stationary because of maintenance, sickness, or complacency. There will be days when you "just don't wanna." If you have a "go, go, go" type of plan, there may come a time when you want to "rest, rest, rest." You will need to listen to your mind and body when these days happen because your health is always going to be a huge factor in your overall success on the road.

What will you do when the weather is bad? You might have a day of hiking washed out by unexpected thunderstorms. You may plan to do some maintenance but find yourself unable to do so on a foggy day. Things will not always go as planned, and sometimes the impeding factor is the weather itself. You will likely not want to spend the day confined in your van, which means you'll need to learn how to play along with Mother Nature. Not only will you need a solid weather app, but weather gear, as well. There are certain points in the United States where snow exists year-round. There are also locations where the temperatures can reach over 100 degrees.

Besides being prepared with equipment, make sure you're mentally ready for bad weather, too. If it's going to rain, perhaps you find a local, free museum. If the temperatures are going to be incredibly high, sleep during the day and drive at night to avoid overheating yourself and your van.

Additionally, boredom is real. Finding structure will help you prevent this, but it's going to happen. You might have a daily ritual, but even that will become tedious at times. Even when you find yourself driving to your next adventure, you might find yourself sick of driving and tired of listening to the same old music. This is natural. Don't take boredom as a sign of failure. Instead, pull over and find a new station, podcast, or audiobook. Perhaps you can take some time to catch up on your housekeeping and organization. Maybe you pause and write down how you're feeling. Do a search online for somewhere nearby to take a stroll and clear your thoughts.

When you feel this way at home, what do you do? Most likely, you throw on some television, or call your friends, or find something around the house to occupy your time. You can still do these things on the road, too! It's entirely ok to feel burnt out on driving all the time. Allow yourself downtime, and when you find yourself feeling bored of that, seek out new ways to occupy your time. Consider picking up games and activity books or coloring books. What about journaling? If you're a creator, you can still paint, knit, and craft on the road, or dabble in whatever your preferred media is. Anything you can do to occupy your time can be done in a van, as long as you're willing to change the scale. For example, you won't be able to throw an entire pottery wheel and kiln on your van, but you can grab some modeling clay and play with making tiny creations that will exercise your talent and creativity.

Your Wealth

Despite not having fixed bills, van living can be expensive. Prepare for this now. Before you start budgeting — which we'll discuss in another section — you need to know what types of expenses you can encounter. This includes everything from mechanical breakdowns and flat tires, to daily expenses, like gasoline, food, water, and generator operation. Parking permits cost money, and showering on the road can cost money too (if you don't have a water supply onboard). Every cup of coffee you purchase at a gas station dips into your budget.

If you plan to make van living your full-time lifestyle, what will you do for income? Many employers offer the opportunity to work remotely, which can be a huge benefit, depending on your profession. This also means you'll likely need to be sure you have a functioning laptop and a reliable Wi-Fi signal. While more and more public locations offer free Wi-Fi, consider if you'll really want to spend every day in a new coffee shop or home improvement store parking lot borrowing signal in order to send in a big report. Instead, you may wish to invest in a web connection amplifier or booster, so that you can run your office right from your van.

You may instead decide to do freelance work on the road. You'll be surrounded by infinite muses, so if you are able to do so, make it happen! You can also run a blog or livestream your journey. Again, this will require a Wi-Fi signal and likely a handful of equipment, so be sure you have a solid plan in place before you set up your van. Having an adequate workspace in your van will definitely increase your professional success.

Van living is incredibly rewarding; however, it does include a bit of adaptation, especially if you've lived a relatively sedentary, domestic life. You may feel like a proverbial fish out of water for some time, but this does not mean you're "doing it wrong." In fact, it means you're finally spreading your wings and finding your groove.

Advice from The Road- Part 1

I hate to be the bearer of bad news, but everything is going to go wrong. Not necessarily all at once, but don't rule that out!

When we hit the road, we started slowly. We started with a two week trip around the vicinity of our home. We wanted to make sure that, no matter what happened, we would be within a reasonable distance of our actual home, so we could "come back" if everything proved to be too much. That included too expensive, too scary, too unpredictable... if at any point we got overwhelmed, we could dart back home and say we had a very nice, short vacation.

Everything went according to plan. We saw the sights, we took the back roads, we gathered loads of amazing photographs and memories. Then, just nine hours away from home, everything went sideways. Huge mechanical breakdown — one of those situations where one thing breaks, and then all the bits and pieces around it start breaking. It was beyond anything we could take care of ourselves because so many things were just falling apart.

Worse yet — we were supposed to be in a wedding at home in just two days!

We had the choice of trying to find someone who could help fix it, or just abandon our van, find a rental car, and figure out how to get the van back later. It took all day, but we were able to find — and get the van to — a mechanic. Even then, it wasn't fixable without ordering parts that would take several days to arrive.

Thankfully, the mechanic was sympathetic to van life. He'd done it himself. Since he couldn't fix it, he came up with a suitable workaround that would get us home. He also recommended that, once we started driving, we not stop except for fuel.

We thought we were home free but still fell prey to the mayhem that can be road life. Even when you think things are going well, it just takes one situation to remind you that "fine" is a temporary state of mind.

Still, there's nothing I'd give up about life on the road. Bad things happen in an apartment. Your car can break down on the way to the office. Your milk will go bad, and your dog will barf in your shoes.

A Van Lifer is someone who can adapt, overcome, and think of creative situations to nearly every problem. Furthermore, they accept that sometimes the solution is "ask an expert." Van Life is a community effort, even if that community is constantly moving in different directions!

Did we get back on the road? Absolutely! We had to spend a bit more time at home than we planned, getting the parts we needed, but that gave us time to learn more about the situation and research solutions for when (not if) it happened again.

Section 2: Finding Your New Home

Being aware of what it takes to successfully live on the road is all well and good, but once you have your mind made up, it's time to find the chariot that will carry you through all of life's adventures.

Again, you might take to the internet to find pictures of vans with white-washed walls, gleaming hardwood floors, tile backsplashes, and even wood-burning stoves. Looks awfully cozy, doesn't it?

While you can make these beautiful images part of your reality, the truth is that it will take a lot of work to get there.

In this section, we'll look at the different things you need to keep in mind when choosing your new vehicle, as well as how to proceed with converting your van into your dream home.

Chapter 1: Considerations for Choosing the Right Vehicle

If you look at any Van Life-themed social media account, you'll find that the term "van" is somewhat open to interpretation. You'll see a fair share of classic vans, such as Volkswagen Vanagons, Westphalia, and Transporters. You'll also see conversion vans, cargo vans, and European camper vans. But the lifestyle also extends to "skoolies," or converted school buses. This, in turn, has inspired folks to convert buses of all kinds. Inventive folks have also taken to converting campers from part-time vacation homes to full-time homes on wheels.

So, when you start searching for your new home, you might be completely stalled at how many options are available. In a nutshell, your decision will be driven by a lot of personal factors. Let's examine these further.

Determining Vehicle Size

There's a considerable amount of difference in size between a skoolie and a VW Transporter, just as there's a huge difference between a three-bedroom house and a studio apartment.

One of the first things you'll need to consider is how much space you need. There are a lot of elements that can go into this part of your accommodations.

1. The number of passengers — and their species!
2. The length of the trip
3. The amenities, such as a bathroom, food preparation area, etc
4. Personal preference

The number of passengers will, of course, dictate how many seats and how many sleeping areas you will need in your van. If you'll have children with you, you might feel most comfortable if they're able to be safely belted into fixed seats while the vehicle is moving. While nearly every veteran van lifer has an amusing story of using a cooler as a seat, it's frowned upon by the law and definitely not safe!

If you're bringing your Adventure Pup or a Feline Mascot (neither of which is unheard of!), you'll have to plan to accommodate their needs, as well. For dogs, you'll want to make sure you have room for them to rest while you drive, move around as they wish when they're not on an adventure with you, and a spot for them to sleep. This can mean making room for a dog bed or making room in your bed for a dog. Cats typically need around 16–18 square feet of space to feel comfortable. They'll also need a litter pan that won't slosh all over the floor of the van unless otherwise toilet trained. Many people do share their van life with a furry friend, so it can be done, with careful planning!

The second part of determining space from the number of passengers is based on comfort level. If you are currently sharing a three-bedroom house with two children and a dog, You're accustomed to a certain amount of space in which to maneuver. Even in the largest bus, you will still run into each other, and you will find privacy a very rare element, indeed. However, if you're currently sharing a studio with your partner, then you're already well-prepared for the challenges that come with cohabitating in a tiny space.

The length of the trip will also dictate the size of vehicle you need, if largely from the standpoint of accommodating four seasons worth of equipment and clothing. If you plan on making your van your permanent home, then you'll need to consider how you'll plan for the seasonal changes. Perhaps you take the opportunity to "chase the weather" and always park somewhere where the weather is dry and warm. Perhaps you choose a vehicle with additional storage for rain gear, snow gear, heavier blankets or sleeping bags, and fans for hot weather.

If you have the opportunity to stop and regroup periodically through your trip, you won't need to stash as much stuff. If you have a small storage unit (or a friend or relative who's willing to let you borrow some space), you can swing by as the situation calls for to change out your equipment, clothing, and more. Granted, this means you'll have to plan ahead to drive to that specific location in time, but it can save you hundreds of pounds and several square feet of extra "stuff" you don't need to carry with you everywhere.

The next consideration is how you will use the room within your vehicle. If you plan to have a bathroom area, you're likely going to want a camper- or bus-type set up. If you instead plan to pack a portable toilet and bucket-style shower, you can really make any type of vehicle work. We'll discuss this in more detail shortly, but at this stage, you'll want to consider if you want to have a full water closet with plumbing or if you can deal with an alternative plan.

The same is true for food preparation areas. The most rugged vans might have a cooler and a propane burner. The most luxurious have full oven ranges, small refrigerators, kitchen sinks, and cabinets. In between are an almost infinite variety of choices. We'll discuss kitchen needs and practical applications in a later section too, but at this stage, consider how much room you feel will be necessary for the kind of food prep you plan. If you're going to install plumbing, gas, or electricity for this, it's best to think of it now.

Lastly, your own personal preferences are something you truly need to consider. On paper, a solo voyager needs only a driver's seat and a bed, with room for storage. In reality, you might find yourself feeling very claustrophobic. The opposite can be true, too. You might find yourself overwhelmed by the size of your space and the maintenance required to keep it clean and functional.

One practical test that is recommended by all sorts of van life experts is the "try it at home" test. Before purchasing a van, bus, or camper of any kind, look up the approximate dimensions of space within the vehicle. Next, find a space in your home, garage, yard, basement, etc., and tape off those exact dimensions. Some experts recommend hanging sheets or shower curtains to give the illusion of the van walls, but you may be able to get a feel for what you'll be working with without going that far.

Without anything in it, how does this space feel? Now start adding objects to the area, either figuratively by marking off the space with tape or chalk, or literally. How big is the sleeping area? If you take that portion away, how well can you maneuver in the remaining space? There will be a learning curve when you actually start living in a van, but if you feel uncomfortable with the space before it's even "real," then you'll definitely want to consider a different option.

Another thing to keep in mind is the height of the van. If you're going with a regular-style van that does not have a pop-top, you may not be able to stand fully upright in the back. For those who are planning to use the van only as a place to sleep and store things, this might be perfectly acceptable. For others, this might be extremely limiting. Again, this comes down to personal preference, but it is definitely something you'll want to consider before you invest in your new home on wheels.

Vehicle Specifications
Beyond the considerations of space, there is the fact that you will have to drive this vehicle from time to time!

Of course, size is a consideration when operating a vehicle, as well. You should feel comfortable driving your van, camper, or bus in a variety of conditions, including on regular city streets, on the highway, on unmaintained or unpaved roads, and also be able to park and reverse.

While your particular trip might not include all of these elements, there will be times when something unforeseen occurs, and you'll need to make do. For example, there are parts of the country where the detour for a temporarily closed well-traveled road is a dirt path. Additionally, you might find it necessary to hit the freeway to get to the next closest gas station, even if you've carefully planned to avoid cities as much as possible. Therefore, it's important to be able to safely guide your vehicle wherever you happen to roam.

If you plan to frequently encounter those unmaintained and unpaved roads, you'll also want to pay close attention to your drivetrain. A drivetrain contains the parts (components) of a vehicle that deliver power to certain wheels.

Let's look at the differences:

- Two-wheel drive (2WD). If your van is referred to as "rear-wheel drive" or "front-wheel drive," it's a 2WD model.
    - Rear-wheel drive delivers the power to the back wheels, and thus the vehicle is "pushed" forward from behind, so the front wheels can handle steering. Many sports cars are RWD, resulting in a balanced, powerful drive. On the flip side, RWD vehicles perform poorly in wet or freezing conditions.
    - Front-wheel drive delivers power to the front wheels, where the engine weight provides balance that improves overall traction. These vehicles typically have a more respectable fuel economy, as well, which can be important to your budget.

- Four-wheel drive (4WD). This option allows drivers to select between RWD and 4WD, depending on the terrain. 4WD delivers power to all four wheels simultaneously, which is fantastic when taking on tough terrain but terrible for your fuel economy. This is why engineers offer the ability to turn off 4WD when the conditions don't require it.
- All-wheel drive (AWD). This option is becoming more and more popular with larger vehicles. AWD requires a front, rear, and central differential, which means all four wheels have power when they need it. A lot of modern (post-2015) heavy-duty vehicles offer this type of drivetrain as an option. Automatic AWD operates in 2WD until the computer sensors determine extra power is needed in a specific location. It is unlikely that you will find this feature on a bus or older van, however.

The rest of the vehicle options you'll need to choose between are far more intuitive. Do you want an engine that runs on regular gasoline or diesel? Check the specifications for any vehicle you're interested in to determine what kind of fuel it needs, as well as the overall fuel economy.

What about transmission? Can you drive a standard, or will an automatic transmission be the best option for you and any others who will be along for the trip? While fans of each option can debate the merits and downfalls of each for eternity, the reality, in this case, is that you'll need to be able to choose a van you can regularly drive without issue.

Insurance

We won't go into too much detail on this topic because requirements and options vary from state to state and country to country. Still, insurance is a very important part of the equation. Not only will you need to have insurance on your vehicle if you plan to drive anywhere, but you'll want to make sure your contents are covered, as well.

Before you purchase any van, bus, or camper, speak with your insurance representative. You'll want to make sure you're covered not only as a driver but also for any accidents that might befall your new home. There are plenty of situations that might render your vehicle undrivable or your quarters unliveable. You need to make sure you're protected not just on the road but for your lifestyle, as well.

When you speak to your insurance representative, make sure you bring up all of these concerns and receive a quote. You will need to decide if you prefer to budget for a higher level of insurance coverage or put away enough savings as a cushion for any mishaps that occur. While it may seem early to think about this, it's crucial that you are able to afford the insurance on any vehicle you might take out on the road. Otherwise, it's simply not the vehicle for you!

Chapter 2: So Many Choices!

If you were to type the word "van" into Google, you'd probably get far, far more information than you could rationally digest in one sitting. Therefore, we'll quickly run through the different types of vehicles you might consider, as well as some factors that might go into your decision to purchase — or stay far away from — that type.

There are plenty of nuances and adaptations to each and every individual van, so it would be impossible to review every single brand that has ever been used for van life. Instead, we'll look at the overall classes of van, and remember — these are just basic guidelines. As they say on the road, "Your Mileage May Vary!"

Classic Vans

These are your Vanagons, your Westphalia, Transporters, and all of the Instagram-ready VW campers that fit the expected stereotype. This class can also include any pre-1990 vans from any manufacturer.

Speaking from an aesthetic point of view, these vehicles are often very photogenic and will get tons of attention on the road. They've got that "old school" appeal that dredges up pleasant, nostalgic memories in nearly anyone who traveled extensively in childhood.

There is, in fact, a huge community of Classic Van Lifers, so you'll be able to connect with plenty of folks who have extensively driven, maintained, rehabbed, worked on, lived in, or are in any possible way familiar with these vans. This is great news for anyone new to van life because you'll have plenty of resources and support through each step of the process.

In fact, when shopping for a Classic Van, you'll find that a large portion of those for sale will be more or less road-ready, due to the fact that many people have purchased and rehabbed these vehicles, then moved on to a bigger and better project following the success of their maiden voyage.

Also, thanks to the recent resurgence in popularity of these vehicles, it's not too difficult to find information that will guide you through basic repairs and maintenance. Since these are vehicles that are actually driven on the road regularly today, it's not too terribly hard to find spare parts, either.

Being able to handle repairs and find spare parts easily is a good thing because you will likely have to do this with frequency, unfortunately. Older vehicles, no matter how well maintained, are prone to breakdowns. Hoses wear out, parts get bent, you might run too hot or too cold, and things will simply stop working over time. If you choose an older vehicle like a Classic Van, try to get as complete a service history as possible. You might also luck out and find one with a new or refurbished engine, but always inspect all of the mechanical aspects — you never know when one of them is going to show their age.

Another consideration is the maintenance you can't handle on your own. Some of the older, foreign-built vehicles require special tools, parts, or mechanical knowledge. Rather than being able to breeze into any auto mechanic's garage, you will need to make sure someone on staff can repair your year, make, and model of van. A breakdown is always inconvenient, but extra frustrating when you have to spend time and energy figuring out where to go for assistance.

Additionally, things like "fuel efficiency" and "safety technology" are relatively new terms in the automotive world. Unlike today's vehicles, the vans of the 1960s didn't need to meet speed limits of 70 miles per hour regularly. Seatbelts didn't become mandatory until 1968. Airbags didn't become a requirement until 1998. Though Classic Vans are built like actual tanks in many regards, they are — by and large — lacking in the modern technology of current vehicles.

Conversion Vans

A Conversion Van is a type of van that is able to "convert" to a livable space. Early conversion vans of the 1970s simply added extra seating, or seats that folded into beds, and plush features, like carpeting and interior lighting. In the 1980s and 90s, features like televisions, VCRs, and indoor-style outlets were added to the category. Conversion vans are insulated, ventilated, and may be equipped with an isolated battery for a non-engine power source. In many ways, conversion vans are not unlike some of today's standard SUVs. But, even the most well-equipped conversion van will require some adaptation in order to be a full-time home.

Conversion vans are typically not too terribly expensive to purchase or maintain. It's relatively easy to find an older Chevy, Ford, or Dodge conversion van that has decent bones at a decent price. Since these vans are usually based on, very similar to, or completely identical to regular passenger vans, it's easy to find parts, and you won't need to find a mechanic who specializes in your particular van.

Spending less on the vehicle itself means you can allocate more funds toward the customization of the vehicle. It's also very likely that you'll find a Conversion Van that has some of the parts and pieces that you'll want in your finished van. For example, a lot of Conversion Vans have out-ward-swinging doors instead of sliding doors. Many manufacturers use this option as a way to stash fold-out tables or storage, which you can incorporate into your overall van scheme. Many also have built-in storage, which you can expand upon or leave as-is. You'll be able to enjoy seats with seatbelts that then fold into beds, saving you the problem of seats and beds as separate entities.

Some Conversion Vans were created with higher roofs, which may allow you to stand up comfortably but will definitely let you take advantage of more storage opportunities along the walls or roof.

Cargo Vans

Cargo Vans share the same advantages as Conversion Vans when it comes to being regularly maintained. Cargo Vans are being manufactured to this day, often as part of vehicle fleets for commercial and industrial businesses. Typically, Cargo Vans have a completely empty body, aside from a driver and passenger seat. Some have old tool racks, storage cabinets, or hanging storage in the back, depending on what they were used for in their past life. You may choose to incorporate or remove these to start fresh.

One thing that many Van Lifers enjoy about Cargo Vans is that they have very few windows. That means any wall is appropriate for building or storing. That also means you don't have to worry about looky-loos peeping in your van when it's parked or while you're sleeping.

On the flip side, both cargo and conversion vans typically have a lower fuel economy. While most options will function on regular unleaded gasoline, which tends to be less expensive, you will be stopping at fuel stations more regularly. You may also wish to keep spare fuel on hand for emergency situations.

You might find that many of the cargo vans on the market have very high mileage, especially if they were regularly used as part of a business. The advantage to this is that business vehicles are usually well-maintained since they're a crucial part of the operation. Still, you'll want to be prepared for any aging vehicle maintenance requirements that might come up.

Depending on your willingness to invest time and money into the van project, having no basic setup in a cargo van might also be a disadvantage. After all, you will need to create a liveable space out of nothing. You can find rehabbed cargo vans for sale, but these will cost more than a completely blank slate, of course. We'll talk more about what it takes to rehab and fully construct a living space in a van in the next chapter, but this is definitely something to keep in mind at this stage of the game, as well.

Euro Vans

First, bear in mind that the term "Euro Van" can refer to two different things. First, a Volkswagen Eurovan is a very specific make and model of van. These pop-top vans were offered in the US between 1993 and 2003, and many are still around and functional today.

There are others who refer to any European touring-style van as a "Euro Van." This can include Mercedes Sprinters, Klassen vans, Fiat Ducato, Renault Trafic, and other vehicles manufactured overseas. With the exception of the Mercedes Sprinter, it's not often you'll find these types of vans in the United States; however, with the growing market for off-grid options, more and more are arriving stateside.

When you're shopping for anything under the umbrella of "Euro Van," double-check if it's an actual VW Eurovan or a European van conversion.

Interestingly enough, VW Eurovans and Sprinter vans share a lot of common features. For example, they both are designed with large and small cargo storage options. They're more modern vehicles, which means you don't have to dredge up historical data to learn more about how they work. Additionally, as modern vehicles, they're equipped with smaller engines that are more powerful and consume less fuel.

Of course, there's a downside to this: as European creations, you'll need to find a mechanic who understands the engineering. They can also be difficult to find parts for, and expensive to repair. There will be more technical elements, such as computer systems, while the earlier and older models have more manual aspects.

Additionally, one thing to keep in mind about these taller vehicles is that you will need greater clearance. While this is typically not a problem on well-traveled highways, where semis and commuter buses are expected, this may pose a challenge on some of the more off-the-beaten-path locations you wish to visit. You can also encounter issues with parking garages if you find yourself within city limits.

Buses

There is a lot that can be said about buses, but the three basic options are School Bus, Coach, or Transit. Though the term "Skoolie" refers specifically to School Buses, the community as a whole tends to accept nearly any bus under the umbrella term.

There are significant differences between the three. True Skoolies are very affordable. Retired school buses can be acquired from multiple sources, including junkyard auctions, school district dispersal sales, online auctions, and more. There are several different lengths and configurations available as well.

Coach buses are bigger and bulkier than school buses, but they have one significant advantage: Uunder-cabin storage. If you've ever traveled the country by bus, you'll recall stowing your bags under the bus at the curb. This is great if you want to take along bicycles or large gear, or need to pack for all seasons. The size of the vehicle can be somewhat daunting though when navigating narrow city streets or winding mountain passages.

Transit buses are retired city buses. Like skoolies, these can come in various shapes and sizes. They rarely have the extra storage, but one unique feature is that some smaller city buses are equipped with wheelchair lifts or entry-assist options, which can be very helpful for those with mobility concerns.

Nearly all buses are equipped with a diesel engine, but some will have the engine in front, while others have the engine in the rear. If you're planning on running plumbing and electric wiring, you'll definitely need to mind the engine. You'll also need to know how to access it for repairs and maintenance, and pack the essential equipment, including any ladders or hydraulic lifts you might need.

One major downside to buses is that repair shops are extremely scarce for these vehicles. They tend to be pretty straightforward in their engineering, so it is possible to learn some DIY repair techniques, but if you're not mechanically inclined, you might have a rough time in the event of a breakdown.

Additionally, insurance can be a bit tricky on buses, but not impossible. As mentioned before, speak to your local representative to get the details before you go on a bus buying spree!

Campers

"Campers" is another somewhat ambiguous term. Some people call any van that you can sleep in a "camper." Others consider pull-behind trailers with living quarters "campers." For some, a "camper" is a full RV. Still others consider a "camper" a trailer that contains nothing more than room to sleep and adequate ventilation and weather protection.

There's a huge difference between an Airstream "camper" and a Patriot "camper" and a Vistabule "camper." When searching and shopping, be fully aware of what anything under the generic term "camper" entails.

For the most part, anything with the title of "camper" will be a prefabricated home on the road. It will include sleep areas, food prep areas, seating areas, and storage. There may be a bathroom, depending on the size of the camper. It may be a trailer instead of a combined living/driving space, such as in a van or a bus. Then again, one man's trailer is another man's camper!

When it comes to choosing the type of vehicle you plan to take on the road, there are really no "wrong" answers. While every class of vehicle has its own community that is completely devoted to that particular model, there are advantages and disadvantages to every single one. You'll find that even within these communities, there will be devotees to a certain year, make, or model.

Therefore, it's really impractical to listen to the recommendations of online forums, friends, or family members unless they face the same exact challenges, situations, and preferences as you will. Instead, pay attention to details. What are the dimensions? How many seats? What kind of engine does it have? What does its maintenance history look like? What type of fuel economy does it get? And most importantly — are you going to feel comfortable living in it?

Chapter 3: Ready-to-Roll, or Ready-to-Rehab?

The next consideration for your van home is how much work you want to put into transforming the space inside into the home of your dreams.

Ask yourself these two questions:

Do you want to create the ultimate space, in which you can comfortably live the rest of your life?

More importantly, are you willing to put in months or even years of hard work in order to create that space?

When asked what was most surprising about the process of gutting and rehabbing a van or bus, nearly everyone who has gone through the exercise will say the time of the entire process. When you browse those gorgeous van homes on the internet, see if you can't research the owners or builders to see how long they spent on the process. Many are very upfront with the process of refurnishing it, including all of the challenges that go along with that. After all, Van Life is a community effort!

Though many of the vans and skoolies you see on social media are labors of love, rebuilt from bare bones, you can start with a fully ready-to-roll vehicle. Yes, it will cost you more at the outset, but buying a fully rehabbed and refurbed vehicle means you won't have to strip the inside. You won't have to rewire anything. You won't have to learn practical plumbing. You won't have to create structures. You won't have to source lumber, nails, screws, tools, hinges... nothing! You can simply open the doors to your new home, look around, and decide where you want to put your belongings.

If that sounds like an absolute nightmare, then you are clearly more in the "Do It Yourself" camp. Before you purchase a giant transit bus and start demolition, there are a few things you need to ask yourself:

How much time can you devote each day to construction?

For many, construction starts out as a "little bit each day" type of project, but swiftly becomes a full obsession. There will be setbacks. Things will not work out exactly as planned. You will cut a piece of insulation multiple times, trying to get it to fit along a curved wall... and eventually, you will cut it to the point where you can't use it. You will find that the plumbing absolutely cannot go there, or there, or really anywhere that it might make sense. Every person who has ever changed anything about their van has been in this exact position.

And that is how we become obsessed — this drive to solve all problems immediately takes over all reason. At the same time, you might still be working your day job as you work on your van space. Your partner, your children, your dog and cat, might all be rightfully concerned that you're spending all night in the van.

This is an easy way to burn yourself out on the whole project. As you encounter one frustration after another, you might decide it's not worth it. While we have no practical cures for the difficulties you'll no doubt encounter, it is highly recommended that you work on your van or bus slowly and surely, rather than trying to rush through it. If you're planning a very extensive makeover, don't plan to leave in two months.

A simple rule of thumb: If time is of the essence, choose something that's ready to go (or at least very close). If you want to really create something from the ground up, don't have a deadline.

Can You Build It?

Be very honest with yourself: do you know anything about construction, electricity, plumbing, insulation, drywall, cabinetry, etc.? Or, are you handy enough that you feel very confident about learning? Can you see a straight line, take a variety of accurate measurements, and execute the product in your mind?

There are four main steps to the process of creating your dream space inside a van.

First, you need to gut it. This is especially true if you purchase a bus that still has the seats inside. You will need to remove everything, and you will need to somehow get rid of it or repurpose it.

As a side note, you will need to be creative when it comes to the collection of school bus seats you're about to have if you've gone with a skoolie. Some folks have luck selling them "as is" to people in the area or via online auctions. More likely, you'll want to take them apart and sell the metal for scrap. Unless you have loads of space in which to store dozens of seats, this is something you ought to plan on doing before you bring your skoolie home, too.

Once you've got your open space, you need a functional design. You'll need to consider not just the overall flow, but where you're going to put the heaviest weight loads, where you're going to put storage or built-ins, and the reality of where you can put plumbing or electricity, which might be based on where you put the water source or hook up, generator, or solar panels. You'll need to be aware of where and how the doors open, as well as the windows.

Most people who have completely gutted and refurbished a van report having at least two to three versions of their design plans, so don't be too concerned if your first plan has to be scrapped. Learn, and move on.

Next comes executing the design. You'll need to run any electric and plumbing before you put in insulation and walls. You'll have to put in walls before you build structures, such as cabinets, seating areas, or sleeping areas.

A side note about storage: One of the best ways to maximize storage is to put it under seating or sleeping areas. One very popular trick is to raise the sleeping area as high as you can, to create a larger storage space beneath. You can build the frame of your bed over a cabinet system to create both open and closed storage underneath your bed. Perhaps you add a fold-out table to the base of your bed or seating that pulls out like a drawer. The options are infinite!

As you are constructing your new home, you will need both materials and tools. Of the two, the tools might be the most cost-prohibitive, as well as the hardest to source. You will also make multiple trips to the hardware store each week. Therefore, you must account in your budget for tools, supplies, as well as gas money and time spent at the hardware store acquiring these things. You might see if there is a tool-lending program in your community, as this can save you several hundred dollars. You might also cruise local selling walls to see if there are used tools available in your area. The unfortunate truth about these processes though, is that you might not find what you need exactly when you need it.

Despite all of your best intentions, there will be waste. Anything from bent nails to stripped screws, to perfectly usable lumber cut to the wrong length. You will not want to keep this waste forever, so consider a plan that will allow you to collect, remove, and appropriately dispose of it. This may mean a call to a junkyard or working with your regular waste management company.

Can You Afford It?

The cost figures for fully renovating a skoolie range from $10,000 to $30,000. Granted, that's cost over time, and as mentioned earlier, it can take years to fully construct the space of your dreams.

We've alluded to some of the expenses here, but let's put it all on the table.

You'll need:

- tools
- safety equipment, such as goggles and gloves
- lumber
- screws, nails, hinges, knobs, sliding rails, bolts, and anchors
- wiring
- insulation
- plugs and switches
- pipes
- walls
- countertops/ sealed surfaces
- flooring
- faucets and fixtures for water closet

This doesn't include any decorative items, such as backsplashes or paint, or power and water supplies, which we'll discuss in more detail in the next chapter. It also doesn't include any books, courses, or instruction you might pay for to help you with your endeavors.

Do You Have the Work Space?

If you're going to be working on a vehicle for months or years, you need a space where you can safely and legally do so.

It is unlikely that a skoolie will fit in the garage of your suburban home. It is also unlikely that you'll be permitted to work extensively on demo and re-hab in the parking garage of a city condo building. If you know someone who has a large yard where you can work, that might be a great option... until the neighbors call the city.

There are legal considerations for working on vehicles within some city or corporation limits. Even if you're not disposing of harmful liquids, less enthusiastic neighbors might consider your activities a nuisance. Therefore, you'll want to find a nice, large space — preferably indoors — where you can work on your vehicle. And then a backup location. And possibly even a backup to the backup. Whether you wear out your welcome or simply outgrow your space, you'll need a plan, since you can't just plop a large bus or very tall van down anywhere.

Most beginner van projects are somewhere in between "completely ready" and "completely reconstructed." You might choose a "mostly ready" van, and lift the bed to add storage or shorten the sleeping area to add a food prep area. You might start with only the minimal changes, then add a little room here or include a fold-out table there as you spend time living in your new space.

Alternatively, you might feel that life on the road is not complete unless you have a wood-burning stove, fully functional skylights, and a hand-painted porcelain backsplash in the bathroom. There's nothing wrong with this perspective, either.

Ultimately, creating your van space is a balance between what you *want* to do, and what you *can* do. If there is a significant overlap between the two, then best wishes on your rehab and refurb experience! If you find that you're lacking in time, skill, funds, or space, you might scale back your project. You might wish to find a mostly-ready van or add the assistance of a professional if the issue is time or skill.

The internet is full of experiences shared by those who have made this journey before. We'll share a few links in the **resources guide** to get you started. When it comes to the building stage, however, you truly cannot research too much, especially if you are a novice DIY-er. You'll want to consider safety, practicality, usability, and durability of everything you construct to be 100% sure before you lay the first nail or cut the first board!

And most of all, have patience and faith. Whether or not it turns out exactly as you dreamed, it will turn out exactly as you have built it. Your planning and patience will pay off in the end.

Chapter 4: Budget Considerations for Creating Your Van

While it may seem that we harp and harp on the concept of budget, you'll find that this is with good reason. One of the most common reasons people give up on the van life dream is because they run out of money before they even have the chance to hit the road.

While it's true that you can save quite a bit of money by abandoning regular bills, multiple car payments, mortgages, and the like with the vagabond lifestyle of the road, you will need to invest a bit of money into setting up the lifestyle to be sustainable.

For those who feel cooped up, you might be so passionately drawn to the experience that you feel like you could simply hop in any old van and drive off and "make it work." There is a very specific demographic for whom this is true. If you have plenty of money, the ability to take on any odd jobs no matter where you are, no particular preference about where you sleep at night, a decent cooler, and a reliable propane burner, then it is possible to "make it work."

If you have a family, pets, the desire to have a predictable shower and bathroom experience, the ability to prepare a variety of fresh foods, and the need to sleep in a comfortable bed, then you will need to plan very carefully in the early stages.

So, when it comes to budgeting, we started at the overall "big picture" of all of the various categories of expenses that might come into play. Now it's time to start drilling down into more detail, starting with the van itself.

How Much Will It Cost to Hit the Road?

The equation for determining the overall cost of your van is as follows:

Cost of Vehicle + Cost of Repairs/Rehab/Refurb = Pre-Road Cost

(Cost of oil/oil change x 6) + cost of tires + cost for replacement cost + hourly rate for emergency maintenance = Annual Upkeep Cost

Size of fuel tank x Average Miles Per Gallon = Miles Per Tank
Total Distance Traveled (divided by) Miles Per Tank = Total Number of Fuel Stops
(Size of fuel tank x going rate for fuel) x Number of Fuel Stops = Total Fuel Budget

Pre-Road Cost + Annual Upkeep Cost + Total Fuel Budget is the amount you will need to get you through the first year on the road.

There are ways to maximize your money, however.

First, remember that the bigger the vehicle, the more fuel it will need. Consider purchasing the smallest possible van or bus that you can actually live in. This might require you to do the "try it at home" test a few times with different configurations.

In addition, consider planning your wandering strategically. Instead of California one week and Connecticut the next, consider taking some time to wind along the West Coast. Try finding a good central location where you can park for a longer period of time, and use a bicycle or small motorbike or scooter to explore the sights nearby. This will not only save fuel costs but wear and tear costs on your van as a whole, minimizing maintenance costs. Lastly, if you find a free spot to camp within National Lands, you'll save a significant amount of money on camp fees and site fees while you do this exploration. Another thing to keep in mind when looking at the annual budget is your income. We'll discuss working from the road in more detail shortly, but there are ways to make money while you travel. Any income you make will offset your expenses, of course, and can either go toward regular maintenance and fuel or toward an emergency fund.

Power and Water: The Utilities

There are also some features you can add to the van construction that will help you save, as well. If you add a power supply and water supply, you'll have a fully self-sustaining home on wheels. This means you'll have a lower reliance on stopping at full-service camping parks. You'll be able to produce the power to charge your phones and devices, as well as have a functioning bathroom to help with showers and general clean up.

When it comes to power supplies, the top two options are generators and solar power. Each option has, of course, strong arguments for and against them.

First, let's look at generators:

Pros	Cons
Produce a lot of instant power at any time	Noisy
Not weather dependent	Require fuel and ongoing maintenance
Can handle a lot of wattage	May be prohibited in some locations due to fumes

Now let's look at the argument surrounding solar power:

Pros	Cons
No fumes, no noise, no maintenance	Does not create a lot of power
Can be repositioned as necessary	Power supply is dependent upon intake/ positioning
No on-going expenses: install and done	Can be damaged, which requires replacement

All said, it boils down to your personal preference and budget. A generator will be an ongoing expense but will be able to supply great quantities of instant power. This might be a greater advantage than disadvantage if you're going to need to power a laptop, phone, and WiFi hotspot. On the other hand, if you won't need tons of power all the time, solar panels might be a real budget-saving option.

There are Van Lifers who live without power. You can choose this route as well. Between independent battery charge units, USB plugs in more modern vehicles, and the old-fashioned type of plug that uses a decommissioned cigarette lighter port, it's possible to keep a cell phone charged. You can also take breaks at fast food restaurants, rest stations, or laundromats, and mooch a little power while you fuel your own body, shower, or catch up on some laundry. Before you help yourself to some power, make sure it's allowed. It also probably goes without saying, but never leave your phone unattended, as it will very likely take a voyage of its own. And if you're going to borrow a little electricity, it's considered good road manners if you make a purchase while you're there.

The next consideration is the water supply. If you are going to carry your own water supply, you'll need two tanks — one for freshwater, and one for greywater. Most experts recommend each tank hold up to 5-7 gallons. The main factor in deciding how big of a tank you want is how much you can carry yourself, as you'll be responsible for filling, maintaining, and emptying these tanks. One gallon of water weighs approximately 8 pounds, for reference. Therefore, a five-gallon tank will be a heft of close to 50 pounds, once you include the weight of the tank itself.

You'll also want to make sure that any tank, pipes, or tubing involved with your freshwater supply is FDA-rated as food safe.

Greywater tanks do not have to be food-safe, but are just as important. "Greywater" refers to wastewater from your sink, shower, etc.

You'll want to make sure that both your freshwater and greywater tanks are both accessible and secured, so they are equally available for filling and emptying, and don't slosh around while you drive.

If you're looking for a very simple way to access freshwater, consider the gravity method. This basically involves installing the water supply in a way that gravity delivers the water through the tubing, to your waiting hands, cup, bucket, or wherever you need the water to go. Many rudimentary van shower systems use this method by hanging the water supply over a door or from an overhead hook, and releasing a valve so the water flows freely.

For those who wish to have more control over water flow, a manual hand or foot pump can be installed. Hand pumps require very little mechanical know-how and involve a temporary or fixed pump being added to the open end of the freshwater tank. The design is not unlike a soap or lotion bottle pump dispenser, only on a larger scale. Foot pumps will require a directed flow via a faucet and sink so that the greywater tank catches the runoff and waste, but they offer excellent control over how much water is dispensed at a time.

Lastly, there's the option of an electric water pump. For this option, you will likely prefer a generator that you can run at least part-time to assist with the process, as you'll need at least 12 volts of electricity. With this choice, you do have the option to install a water heater so that you'll have continuous hot water, as well. You can also add an accumulator, which will store a little water each time the water is turned on. The accumulator will let you use a bit of water even when the power is off, which will save on noise and expense.

Then there's the toilet. Technology has come a long way in this regard, so your van won't have to be as primitive as you fear... unless, of course, you want it that way. There are a variety of road-ready commodes available that can be incorporated into your new abode with or without plumbing.

First, there are composting toilets. These toilets are chemical-free and store your waste until you can dispose of it. The secret is a peat mixture and a dehydration process. The liquids go into a separate bottle, which can be dumped securely, while the solids mix with the peat and turn into safe compost. These toilets do require power in order to work, however, as most include a small fan that keeps the process working. Composting toilets can be very expensive, but a very wise investment for those who wish to use the toilet indoors with the most minimal need for chemicals, hassle, or interacting with the resulting matter.

Then there are portable potties. These are small, self-contained toilet units that can be installed anywhere. They feature a waste tank and a water tank and can be "flushed" like a standard toilet, although what's flushed will await future disposal in the appropriate tank. This means that chemicals should be used to keep odor at bay between emptyings, though eco-friendly chemicals are also readily available. These toilets do use a considerable amount of water and can get heavy depending on how long you go between emptying.

Those traveling with children or in groups may want to invest in a full electric camper-style toilet. While impractical to install on a smaller van, this format is suitable for buses, where a waste tank can be stashed under the vehicle and dumped appropriately in waste stations at campgrounds. The benefit here is that you don't have an immediate or urgent worry about overflow, no possible spillage, and the toilet is a permanent part of your home. The downside is that it will have to be incorporated and installed, thus taking up valuable space and requiring a sizable investment.

There are also a variety of low-tech options. From what amounts to a stool with no seat, to a bucket with a seat on it, many Van Lifers have made the most of an awkward situation with a practical — if not at all glamorous — solution. There are multiple small battery-operated or hand-pump style toilets on the market as well, but bear in mind, these are often very low to the ground and still require regular and frequent emptying. Also, consider the fact that you may need to use this device at any hour of the day, in all kinds of weather. Make sure you choose a toilet option that you'll feel comfortable with at midnight during a thunderstorm!

It is possible to live without any plumbing whatsoever, of course. Water can be found in many places, and it's very simple to stock up on gallons of usable drinking water. This will, however, require room for storage. A cooler is a multi-level solution when it comes to water usage, as well. The ice used to keep food fresh in a cooler will, over time, melt. While you might not want to use that water for drinking, you can heat it up with your propane burner and a pot, and enjoy a bath or shower. You can also use that melted ice water to cool off when temperatures are climbing. Toilets can be found at gas stations, restaurants, grocery stores, campgrounds, parks, and rest areas.

When disposing of greywater and waste, it is crucial that you do not contaminate any water sources. Make sure you only dump wastewater in approved and appropriate areas. Composting toilets are less dodgy since the waste has been decontaminated naturally, but some toilet solutions include chemicals that can poison humans and wildlife, and destroy native plants and soil. Whenever possible, use biodegradable, environmentally friendly soaps, cleaners, and toilet papers.

If you choose to go the "natural" route, remember to be courteous. Step away from main areas — even if you're camping on free land, you can still avoid areas where people are likely to walk. Dig your waste trench at least six inches deep, and be sure to bury everything thoroughly once you're done.

Chapter 5: The Search Process

Once you've got all of your plans in hand, it's time to make them so. You know what size vehicle you need and likely have a top-three selection of the type of vehicle you'd like to purchase. You are confident about what you want to put in your van or bus, where it's going to go, and what you need to do to make it happen.

Now stack all of those plans neatly, and throw everything on the floor except your budget.

Shopping for your van or bus or camper can be agonizing if you have very specific requirements. You may choose to wait until you are able to locate The Exact Perfect Vehicle for your adventure. Alternatively, you may choose something that is more of a compromise on your exact requests but meets all your requirements. The choice is entirely your own.

The internet is a fantastic place to find Van Life resources. As a community that has no physical footprint (or rather, one that is always in motion), there are many forums and sites where van dwellers meet up to share thoughts, ideas, and ask each other questions. In fact, we've included some of these in the **resource section** of this book.

As you read through these forums, you'll find discussions about particular types of vans or skoolies, as well as sales ads. Some people within the van community make a fair living off rehabbing and selling vehicles. Others find that they "outgrow" their van and are ready to step up to a bigger, more off-road capable, or in some cases, more frugal vehicle.

Another online resource is vehicle sales sites. Again, we've compiled a few suggestions to get you started in the **resource section**. There are sites dedicated to vans and buses, but you can also find some good deals on regular automotive sites, especially if you're looking for a cargo or conversion van that you can take down to the bare floor and remodel into your own.

There is some debate as to whether it's worth it to reach out to regular car dealerships. The answer is yes. Shopping for a van is not unlike shopping for any other specialty item, like antique glass or rare book printings. You never know where they're going to turn up. You might find just the right base vehicle has come into a dealership as a trade-in and swipe it up before they list it on an online auction. One benefit to this plan is that dealers seldom let vehicles leave their lot without at least a full inspection. Though they might not take the time, or invest the money into fixing anything that's out of sorts, they'll at least be aware and disclose this information to you. Auctions are another great resource, if you're ok with buying vehicles "as is." You might not know its issues, problems, or need for repairs until you get it home and start truly inspecting it, but the vehicle you purchase at an auction can be extremely cheap.

Online auctions have similar perils — you are relying on the word of the person selling the vehicle, and you may not be able to physically inspect the vehicle until you have already paid for it. Still, online auction sites can bring great luck to those who have done their homework and are ready for just about anything.

If you're specifically looking for a bus, you can reach out directly to the source for more information about obtaining one of their decommissioned vehicles. For skoolies, you can reach out to the school district. Frequently, their vehicles pass through local auto auctions, but it's possible the school district might be interested in making a deal, for the right price.

When it comes to coach-type buses, you might need to do a bit more digging. National bus lines will have a point of contact for decommissioned buses, but if you're dealing with a more local outfit, it might require a few calls and emails before you find the right person.

The city transit department will likely have information about what happens to city buses once they're removed from duty. In many cases, they end up in junkyards, auctions, or are donated to various programs, but again, you might be able to make arrangements for purchase first.

When it comes to pulling the trigger and purchasing your vehicle, you must feel fully confident in your decision. You must have addressed all budget considerations, all repair requirements, and be ready to shoulder the burden of any rehab and remodeling that will be needed to make your van or bus your new home.

We encourage everyone to do as much research as possible. Find a handful of options. Decide what things you can compromise on and what features are absolute necessities. Can you wiggle on price? What if you find a vehicle that has higher mileage than you'd like, but the price is perfect, and it's been well-cared for? It is highly unlikely that you'll find a vehicle that meets all of your needs precisely. What is far more likely is that you'll find a vehicle that shows you what features, options, and qualities are really most important to you.

If it is at all possible, try to test drive the vehicle. This might mean doing some traveling. Worse yet — this might mean getting your hopes up, traveling, and discovering it's not going to work.

You will have to feel comfortable driving your new home. In the case of a larger bus, it will take time before driving such a massive vehicle feels natural, but if a simple trip around the block feels desperately uncomfortable for any reason, it might be a good time to head back to the drawing board. There are things that can be altered, improved, or modified, but if you decide you really don't like the way driving a van with a manual transmission feels, it might be less expensive to check out options with an automatic transmission, rather than replace the entire system.

You'll also want the opportunity to really inspect the vehicle in detail. This means you might have to take a crash course in the year, make, and model of the vehicle you're going to check out, but it's better to be fully informed than guessing.

Additionally, see what maintenance and repair records you can get your hands on. The more you know about this particular vehicle's history, the more you can plan for future issues — or at least identify what needs your immediate attention.

Advice from the Road- Part 2

When it came to purchasing our first van, I was adamant that it would have a kitchenette, or at least a purposed food-prep area with storage and running water. My plans for the interior included a fold-out table, which I could use as a work station during the day, and could do extra duty as an eating surface, a drying rack for dishes and laundry, or a spot where we could hang out and play games or plan the next leg of our voyage.

I wanted an automatic transmission. I wanted a vehicle no more than 25 years old. I was fine with higher mileage, as long as it was well-cared for and didn't come with any major problems. I didn't care about color, and I wasn't fussy about how the sleeping area was set up.

We ended up with a VW Vanagon from the 1980s. It did not have a kitchen area. It didn't have a fold-out table. It didn't have so much as a shelf. In the back was a platform and a mattress... that's it.

Instead, it had a recently replaced engine. It had been regularly serviced for the past 30 years. It had only had two owners and still had its original owner's manual (which is roughly the same size as a 1980s phone book, by the way). It came with a automatic transmission, as he hoped, and a gaudy peace sign sticker... which actually hid a deep ding in the side of the door.

Was it the van I had planned on purchasing? Absolutely not. Was I completely wooed by its mechanical soundness, ease of operation, and blank-slate space? Very much so.

We looked at several dozen vans. Some of them we just courted online until the inevitable Huge Issue came to light. We had the chance to kick some of the tires. But when we found this van, two states away, in a heated, climate-controlled garage, I knew that this was the main contender for our future home on wheels.

Section 3: Creating and Maintaining a Budget While on the Road

There are so many factors that go into both creating and maintaining a budget while you're on the road. Here we'll attempt to walk through the process in easy-to-handle pieces.

If you've even started considering your Van Life budget, your head is probably a whirlwind of figures, with questions like:

1. What can I afford to spend each month?
2. What splurges or luxury items will I allow myself?
3. What happens if I run out of money?
4. If I buy this item now, will it cost me more or less in the long run?
5. What'll I do in an emergency? (Followed by feelings of desperation and panic, usually.)

First, take a deep breath. Having an emergency while on the road is really no different than having an emergency at any other time of your life. You can't completely prepare for everything, and while it's going to be deeply inconvenient, you'll have to take everything step by step to move in the right direction.

As for the rest of the questions, we'll address them one by one. While we can't actually sit down with you and do the math for your particular situation, we can bring you some key points and advice from folks who have been on the road, to help you decide where to spend money, where to save money, and where to make money.

Advice from the Road: Part 3

When we first took our van out, we had nothing. Ok, that's not entirely true. We had a bed, tons of really intuitive storage, a large ice-vault type cooler with a valve on the side to empty out the water, and a propane burner with two fuel tanks. Our van didn't even have interior lights until we removed the non-functioning air conditioning unit and accidentally reconnected something.

We thought this was the best way to save money — live as basically and frugally as possible, right? Barebones means no waste, little investment, and a smaller budget. Well, it turns out that we accidentally sabotaged ourselves with this mindset.

We stocked up on what we considered "van food" beforehand. As experienced campers and hikers, we assumed we'd want to eat the same sort of thing in the van that we ate while camping. We thought we were brilliant.

Well, it turns out that, when you're parked in a camp park full of families grilling huge, juicy steaks, that dehydrated chicken curry packet doesn't look so appetizing anymore. Even worse, because your home has wheels, and because you can get an internet signal nearly anywhere, it is very, very tempting to find yourself at the local famous restaurant every night. Which would you prefer: a powdered camping meal or authentic mole enchiladas served by a woman who has her family's 300-year-old recipe?

It's easy to make excuses, too. After all, you're on the road to experience the world as it is, and that includes the local flavor — literally. Problem is, eating at restaurants eats your budget right up!

So, you learn to compromise. Head to local markets and grocery stores, and stock up on local products there. We could buy all the flavors we couldn't find at home and take them with us wherever we went.

We did have to change the cooler setup, though. We thought we were being budget-conscious by getting the less expensive cooler. Unfortunately, we ended up wasting a lot of food when it got "drowned" in the melting ice.

As a result, we had to modify our entire setup. Just for food? No — to make the most out of our budget. Our no-power, no-water setup was tweaked into a solution that actually reduced our spending. We use only three 160-watt solar panels, which connect to four batteries. These also keep us working while we're on the road. We no longer have to stop at cafes or restaurants and buy something for the privilege of "borrowing" electricity and WiFi — we're self-reliant. (Think about it — even if you just buy a $3 snack each day for an hour of guilt-free power, that's $90 a month, and that's with a very low estimate!)

Even better, we have far less food waste. We invested in a more expensive cooler, which plugs into the van's cigarette lighter socket while we're on the road and can connect with the solar battery converter when we're not in motion. Just in case, we have several cooler packs that don't leak, spill, or otherwise ruin our food. We also have a full series of BPA-free food storage containers of all sizes, so if we do need to temporarily run on ice, we lose nothing.

Do we still try out local cuisine at restaurants? Sure, from time to time. But choosing to be able to store and prepare our own fresh food is a decision that required a little more spending on the front end but has saved us literally thousands of dollars each month!

Chapter 1: Determining Your Budget

At its core, a budget is simply a balance between money you have and money you need (or want) to spend. When you live in a fixed, permanent location, it's pretty easy to see what you have, what you need, and what to expect from month to month. After all, our daily routines rarely change overall — and that's why the road is calling to you!

Still, there's something to be said for predictability. Most of us rest easier with at least some perceived control over our daily, weekly, and monthly expenses.

It may feel, at first, like heading out on the road is going to be a complete upheaval of your way of life. In many ways, this is true. But there are plenty of things that aren't going to change about your lifestyle. You'll still need to eat every day. You'll still need to drink plenty of water. You'll still have dirty laundry.

We've included a chart that includes some common ongoing expenses. Bear in mind that this chart only includes expenses that you'll encounter on a continuous basis—we'll get to the start up and packing expenses in a moment.

This is, of course, just a guide to get you started. If you have children on the trip, some of these categories might change a bit. The maintenance for any equipment you install, such as toilets, generators, hot water heaters, and such, will be dependent on what type of equipment you choose and its specific requirements. If you have a pet, you'll need to take their needs into consideration. However, this chart should get you started in the process of thinking about what you need on a running basis.

Expense Category	Considerations	Your Calculation
Fuel	Price per Gallon Miles per Gallon Distance Traveled Fuel Cost Fluctuations (by location) Emergency Fuel Supply	
Maintenance	Oil changes (5-10,000 miles) Tire rotation (5-7,000 miles) Air filter Fluids (Radiator, Transmission, Coolant, Brake, Air Conditioning, Washer, Power Steering) Glass Cracks Windshield Wiper Blades	
Location	Parking pass Camping pass Park entry fees Showers Hotels (if necessary) Greywater dump fees (charged at some campsites)	
Kitchen Supplies	Drinking water Food/Groceries Cleaning tools	

Health	Toiletries (shampoo, toothpaste, soap, etc.) Vitamins Medications (both prescription and OTC) First Aid supplies (bandages, antiseptic cream, cotton swabs) Sunscreen Bug spray Regular medical check-ups, vaccines, dental care
Laundry	Detergent Laundromat costs
Entertainment	Entry fees Park passes Restaurants Cafes/Wineries/Breweries/Distilleries/etc. Gifts/games/toys
Other ongoing expenses	Insurance (Medical, Vehicle, etc.) Generator upkeep (if used) Vet bills (if you bring a pet) Credit card bills Van payment (if you take out a loan for the van) Roadside Assistance Program Cell phone bill WiFi
Expenses from Home (applies only if you choose to maintain your home while you're on the road)	Mortgage/rent Electric/gas/water House sitter/tenant Insurance Taxes

When you're filling out these expenses, try to be both practical and generous in your estimates. No matter where you're traveling, the cost of living is largely based on location. A gallon of water that costs 60 cents at one grocery store might cost $1.09 at another store twenty miles away. You can shop around for bargains, but that might cut into your fuel budget. Unless you're able to really sit down and cruise the internet to find deals at local stores and any relevant coupons, try to plan things out.

You might notice that we included "expenses from home." For some van dwellers, it's impossible to break a lease or sell property in time to get on the road. Some actually maintain their homes, so they have a "base" to return to from time to time. They might have a tenant renting the home or sublease an apartment. If you choose to maintain a stationary home, there will be expenses associated with that location — a mortgage in your name, bills, etc. You'll definitely not want any unpleasant financial surprises while you're on the road, so be sure that you factor in those regular payments if you will have them.

There are also things you can stock up on beforehand, to some extent and expenses that you will only encounter at the start of your trip, and perhaps rarely afterward. Let's take a look at what those might look like.

Expense Category	Considerations	Your Calculation
Emergency Supplies	Storage bin Tarps Bungee cords Duct tape Road flares Jumper cables Tire patch kit Spare gas canister Jack Tool kit	
Camping/Outdoor Supplies	Storage bin Tent/equipment Backpacks Sleeping bags Flashlights/lanterns Batteries Multi-tool	
Health and Wellness	Mirror Tote for toiletries Scissors Towels Storage for dirty laundry	
Bedding	Pillows Sheets Variety of blankets Mattress/sleeping surface Storage for unused bedding	

Kitchen	Large container to store canned/boxed/dry food
	Cooler or refrigerator
	Small containers for open food/leftovers
	Pots and pans
	Cooking tools (spatula, serving spoons, can opener, bottle opener)
	Eating utensils
	Dishes
	Burner or stovetop
	Fuel for cooktop
	Dish bin
	Dishrags

Again, this is not a comprehensive list for every possible scenario, but a few helpful guidelines to get you thinking about what items are part of your necessary routine.

Many of these items will need to be replaced depending on the length of your trip, and in case there is any accidental damage. Overall these will not be things that need to be replaced weekly or even monthly.

Advice from the Road: Part 4
A word about storage.

Everything in your van will need a place to live. Everything.

One of the most challenging parts of living in a van is the fact that you can't put your dirty laundry on a chair and deal with it on laundry day. You can't just let the dishes hang out overnight in the sink. Your van will become very crowded, messy, stinky, and full of pests unless you stash your dirty laundry somewhere, keep your dishes clean and put away, and your surfaces tidy.

Worse yet, if you leave food sitting out, you run the risk of attracting bears, coyote, wolves, and more. While not naturally aggressive, these critters are very interested in any tasty tidbits you might have onboard, and they're naturally equipped with the claws and jaws that will help them get what they want!

When we hit the road, we started with several large bins:

- *One for our emergency supplies, which we labeled the Oh S**t Kit*
- *One for the kitchen goods, which included dry foods and all of our kitchenwares*
- *One for our camping gear, so if it got wet or muddy, it wouldn't roll all over the van and make a mess*
- *One for our dirty laundry — trust me, you want something that seals, especially if you're going to be hiking ten miles a day!*

These were each 60 gallon "under the bed box"-style heavy duty bins with lockable lids, specifically chosen to fit under the sleeping area. We could reach under the bed at any time and slide out the bin we needed — which we could identify because they were labeled on all four sides. The labels weren't anything fancy; just a strip of duct tape with the "Kitchen," "Camp," and so on written in permanent marker.

Under the shelf where these large bins lived was a storage area accessed by smaller doors. This had been where the original owner stored his emergency kit. We chose to create 6-quart sized plastic bins with lids to place in this area. They fit perfectly through the small door, and that way, wouldn't roll around or require additional containment.

We each had two — I chose to make one my toiletry kit — I put my shampoo, conditioner, soap, toothpaste, toothbrush, and hairbrush in one bin. That way, whenever we stopped at a place that had showers or ran into a rest stop to brush our teeth and wash our faces, I didn't have to pick and juggle what I needed — just grab the box and go. And since it had a lid, I didn't have to worry about things falling out and getting lost. If you've ever had a toothbrush fall on a rest area floor, you know that sinking feeling in your stomach when you lose an important piece of equipment!

My second bin held what I considered my daily necessities: medication, a spare phone charger, hair ties, the muscle rub I put on at night, dry shampoo, hand lotion, lip balm, sunburn cream, and my mobile TENS unit. I also had a small bottle of air freshener in there, for that "we really need to make today laundry day" vibe.

When it comes to living in a van, space is at a premium. You don't want things rolling around while you're driving, and you don't want to search all over the place when you're looking for something. If you can create a storage solution for every major area of your daily life, you'll make life so much easier for yourself.

You just have to remember to put everything back where you found it!

Chapter 2: Sticking to It

Now that you have an idea of what your expenses are going to look like, you've got to put some guidelines in place to help you stick to this plan. You know yourself best of all, so if you feel like there will be some moments of excess — such as visiting your favorite theme park or splurging at a restaurant you've always wanted to visit — make sure you add these into your budget at the outset. Just like when you lived in a stationary home, you want to make sure you have as much control over your money as possible.

There are many things you can do to keep your budget low, but you'll have to do some research and planning to carry out these options.

For example, making your own food is going to be considerably less expensive than eating at restaurants several times a week. But, as mentioned in Advice from the Road: Part 3, you'll need to be adequately prepared. Living on ramen every night is neither enjoyable nor nutritious. Make sure you incorporate methods for storing canned, boxed, and dry food, as well as produce, proteins, juices, leftovers, and other things that need to be kept chilled. This way, you'll be able to create healthful, tempting, budget-friendly meals without wasting food. We'll provide some tips on this topic in a later chapter.

Another place where you can save loads of money is by scouting out free parking and camping. Your online van community is possibly the best resource for finding a free place to catch some rest with travelers sharing some of their favorite spots for anyone who is currently on the road.

While there is nothing wrong with pulling into a paid campsite for the night, it can start to eat away at your budget. Many campsites require a $20-$40 per night camping fee, and if they have any extra perks, like vault toilets, WiFi, electricity, water hookups, laundry, or showers, there might be an additional fee to use those services.

Whenever possible, consider finding free camping. In the United States, National forests and wildlife areas and land owned by the Bureau of Land Management, they welcome free camping — as long as the land isn't privately owned. You'll need to do your homework in order to discover these spots, however, and there are several areas where there simply aren't public lands. We've included a few links in the **resource section** to guide your search.

Staying Green is another way to keep expenses down. This includes things like choosing reusable rags over paper products. Using as little water as possible for cleaning and reusing your greywater in practical ways or other options. If you use a generator, consider running it as little as possible. Try solar-powered flashlights — they can charge in the sunshine on your dashboard during the day and light up the van at night. If you don't need to be in motion, stay parked.

Anything you can do yourself saves you an expense, too. This includes maintenance and repair of nearly everything that's in your van or skoolie. If you can learn to perform minor mechanical repairs, you'll only need to pay for parts. If you can repair your own clothing, you won't need to replace it. If you have a roof rack and a sunny day, perhaps you save your quarters on a dryer and air dry your laundry.

Lastly, it's not a bad idea to sign up for fuel perks or discount programs, especially at national chains. Fuel is going to be a constant expense, and if you have the ability to earn discounts, you'll certainly be able to take advantage of them. You might also choose a credit card program through a gas station that provides discounts on fuels and products purchased from that chain. You may also stock up on gift cards for particular gas stations — some of them offer heavy discounts if you purchase gift cards in bulk. Investigate all of your opportunities to save on fuel, since you'll have absolutely no way of predicting what a gallon of gas will cost from one day to another!

Chapter 3: Earning Income While on the Move

If Van Life is to become your full-time lifestyle, you'll need either a very large amount of money before you hit the road, or you'll need regular income. More and more van dwellers are choosing to work while they're on the move. This can take on many shapes.

1. After completely rehabbing and rebuilding a van, you might find you're rather handy. Whenever money runs low, you go into a town, advertise as doing handy jobs, and make a few bucks.

2. You keep going until your funds drop below a certain limit. At that point, you pull into a semi-permanent camp park and get a job in town for a few months. You continue to live in your van, but you show up at the worksite, put in your hours, and let the income accumulate until you reach a comfortable spot where you can pick up and start driving again.

3. You keep your current job and work from the road. Many corporate-type jobs are allowing employees to telecommute from home or other alternative work environments. Your employer might require you to be signed on or otherwise reachable by phone and email during certain times of certain days, so you'll

need to plan wisely to have a reliable WiFi and phone signal during those times.

4. Freelancing is another career path that is gaining in popularity. Again, you'll need a fairly continuous WiFi signal and phone connection, but if you have a talent, you might check popular contracting sites for jobs you can accomplish anywhere you choose to be.

5. The Internet. We live in an age where you can get paid for talking about yourself on the internet. If you're a talented writer, photographer, videographer, or have the gift of gab, you can consider blogging, a YouTube channel, or a podcast. You'll have the ability to charge for ad space and make money by posting sponsored ads.

There are, of course, other types of income opportunities, but the main purpose of these examples is to help you appreciate that you don't have to be a trust fund baby or have millions in the bank before you hit the road.

Depending on the lifestyle you hope to lead, the compromises you're willing to make, and the skills you're willing to learn, anyone can hit the road at any time. It's just a matter of making sure you're very prepared for all of the possibilities and realities.

Advice from the Road: Part 5

I actually started my freelancing career from the road. Because I didn't want to spend the time and effort of sending all of my friends and family post-cards, I started a blog. As I was blogging, my friends would read about my adventures and share the link with their friends, and so on.

After a while, I started getting contacted by people who liked my writing style. They would have little writing projects they needed help with, and would I mind helping them out for a few bucks? Soon, I was devoting about an hour a day to these road projects.

I didn't plan to make money while on the road, but WiFi, Google Docs, PayPal, and the like make it super easy to gain a few bucks here and there. It wasn't long before I realized this was a real passion of mine, too!

Section 4: Preparing for Your Trip

We've discussed some of the preparations in earlier sections, but this one is designed to help you get really road ready. From this section you'll be able to not only make a checklist of things to pack but have places to pack them, and an orderly system for loading and unloading everything you've got. Furthermore, when things go sideways, you'll be prepared with alternatives!

Chapter 1: Your Utilities

When you were building or buying your van or skoolie, you made some very important decisions about things like power, water, toilets, showers, and more. Here is where you make sure you're ready to hit the road with all of these things!

For your power supply, both generators and solar power have special considerations. Do you have all of the knowledge and necessities to keep your generator in good, functioning order? What is your plan for running your generator? What happens if your generator goes out? You should always have a backup plan, such as flashlights and meals that don't require heating (or a heating source that doesn't require power). Does your toilet run off the generator? That's another possibility you'll need to consider.

Where are you going to get your water? Where are you going to dispose of your greywater? What if you run out of water? What are you going to store your water in? What happens if that storage tank gets damaged?

Much like you probably have a plan at home for what to do if the power goes out or a sewer main breaks, you'll need similar alternatives when you're on the road. At the same time, your storage space will be at a premium, so whatever you choose must be as simple as possible. If you are traveling with a family, for example, perhaps the path of least resistance is checking into a hotel for the night while you repair and re-sort all of the equipment that needs attention. If you're on your own, perhaps you stay put for the night, pitch a tent, and make the most of the situation.

Chapter 2: Sleeping Arrangements

When you were building your van or buying your van, you designated space for sleeping. Now that you've built your nest, it's time to feather it!

Your bed is actually a very important part of the van life experience. After all, if you sleep poorly, you might experience unnecessary back and neck pain, or become tired more easily, or just feel generally foggy and groggy. None of these are helpful when you are supposed to be driving or having adventures.

At the same time, it's generally not practical to have a king-sized thermal adjustable massaging bed installed in your van! Thankfully, there are plenty of options on the market when it comes to creating a sleeping environment that will be comfortable for you.

Start with a solid, flat, even base. Then add a mattress layer. Because you're working in a van, you might not be able to just wander into a mattress store and grab a standard commercial mattress. Instead, you might have to do some tailoring.

Futon mattresses tend to be a great medium for the base of your mattress layer. They're designed to be rolled up or folded, so if you need to stash your bedding while you drive, a futon mattress will not be offended. They're also typically stuffed with foam or padding. This means that if you cut into one to make it the right size, you can always just adjust the dimensions of the stuffing and sew it back up. Yes, this will require a little sewing skill, but it doesn't necessarily have to be gorgeous — just rugged and functional.

One thing to keep in mind with this type of mattress is that it isn't necessarily intended to be slept on every night for long periods of time. Do your research as you shop to find one that will be durable, and take care to flip and rotate your mattress often to ensure it wears evenly.

Another option is an inflatable mattress. If you need to use your sleeping area for other functions during the day, an inflatable mattress can be deflated and stashed in a relatively small area. The only downsides to this is that you will need to re-inflate it every time you use it, and it is possible for an air mattress to get tiny rips and holes that will need to be repaired in order for you to continue using it. Furthermore, you'll need to make sure the mattress fits within the dimensions of your sleeping area. Still, there are some very sturdy and comfortable air mattresses available.

On top of the mattress layer, you can add a variety of orthopedic and temperature regulating pads, which are available at most department stores and discount stores. A simple "egg-crate"-style pad might do the job, or you might want to find something that's more sturdy, firm, and will balance out your mattress. Make sure the padding you choose can be sized to your mattress, and if you're going to roll it up and store it when it's not in use, make sure it doesn't create too much unnecessary bulk. Some of the padding on the market might be as thick (or thicker!) than your mattress which could cause storage issues.

You might also consider getting what is affectionately termed a "bug bag" if you choose a non-inflatable mattress, especially if you plan to spend a lot of time in the true wilderness. This is a waterproof, insect-proof, crumb-proof mattress cover, which typically zips to keep the mattress truly protected from all of the elements. This might seem like an unnecessary extravagance until you knock over your water bottle onto your bed in the dark or find a swarm of ants casually enjoying a crumb of food you didn't realize you dropped. If you tailor your mattress to fit the space, it might not be a perfect fit, so buy a size bigger than whatever your mattress started as. You can always use bands or clips to keep it from rustling around as you sleep. Additionally, you'll be able to store your rolled-up mattress and pad in this if necessary.

Next comes the bed sheets and linens. Go with what makes you comfortable, but doesn't require a ridiculous amount of storage. You might see glorious social media pictures of van beds stacked with throw pillows. If you need throw pillows to be physically or mentally comfortable — get them. For the most part, however, you'll need enough pillows to keep your body comfortable, a fitted sheet to keep everything together, and some assortment of blankets for your preferred sleeping temperature.

Keep in mind that temperature can be a hard thing to regulate in a van, especially if you will not have a power source. You may choose to use your sleeping bag in colder climates, or if you're going to be in hotter locations, a light sheet or nothing at all. If you enjoy sleeping with a comforter in a climate-controlled house with a fan blasting directly at you, your sleeping situation might change once you're on the road.

This is another scenario where doing a test run in your garage, basement, or corner of a room will be a good idea. Set up your mattress, pad, and all the accessories you'd like to try. See how it feels, and adjust as necessary. This way, when you finally get out on the road, you'll be in a comfortable, familiar bed.

Remember also that your sheets and blankets will have to hang out in your van. Eventually, they will need to be washed and changed. You might want to have a spare set of sheets on hand and put the used sheets in with the dirty laundry. The goal is to be minimalist, but you need to be practical, as well. If you're the type of person who can wash and dry their sheets as necessary, then you'll be able to get away with just one set.

If you do choose to bring extra bedding, make sure you store it in a sealed container or bag. If you plan on going on any outdoor adventures, you will find that mud, sand, dirt, rocks, and snow will get everywhere. Make sure your clean linen stays clean until you're ready to use it by keeping it stowed away.

Another thing to consider when it comes to sleeping and bedding is windows. Yes, windows.

If you have a skoolie, you may have a lot of windows. That can be a huge advantage because you can open them at night and let the soft night air cool you while you sleep. In addition to the night air, however, you'll also let in the insects, pollen, falling leaves and seed pods, small intelligent rodents, and any looky-loos who might want to peep the interior of your home. All of these are incredibly irritating.

For windows that you'd like to keep open, you'll want to consider screens. You might have to make these yourself. Buy the kits for this at hardware stores. The best part is they don't take much work. You'll have to decide if you want to permanently install the screens or fashion them so they can be popped in when the windows are open. The second option is going to be most convenient, but less secure. A particularly clever rodent or curious person could figure out how to pop them right back out.

What about privacy windows? If you're living in a van, it's highly likely that you have a large rear window. Tinting it for privacy is possible, but be warned that different states have different laws on how dark windows can be. Instead, you might wish to fashion a privacy curtain that can be pulled across the window at night. You can install an actual curtain or use Velcro strips adhered around the van window to hang a blanket or other fabric across the window.

When thinking about window covering, remember that anything you have in the van will get dusty and dirty (maybe even smelly!). The insides of your windows will also gather condensation from your breath as you sleep on cool nights, so make sure your window treatments aren't going to be spoiled by getting slightly damp.

Your main goals for creating your sleep setting will be comfort, climate, the ability to stow and set up quickly and easily, cleanliness, and a sense of privacy. Together, these elements can't necessarily guarantee you a perfect night of sleep, but they'll certainly help!

Advice from the Road: Part 6

The first night in our van, I imagined that everyone was looking in on me. I tried to hide with the blankets over my head, but it was so hot. Eventually, I started feeling more and more comfortable with leaving the windows cracked, and then fully open.

That's when the mosquitos came out. Great big, blood-sucking mosquitos. The van was absolutely filled with them, buzzing all night, feasting on our faces. Even in the mountains, where there was snow, they still came to visit.

We quickly put up makeshift screens in the windows, but it wasn't long before the bugs found all the holes. Our next investment was perfectly-sized screens, which we affixed to the window frame with large, industrial-strength Velcro strips. The screens stowed neatly behind the driver's seat, and extra Velcro is an easy investment.

The result was a quiet night of sleep with peaceful mountain breezes and no bug attacks!

Chapter 3: Storage Solutions

Much like power sources, storage solutions are something we've touched on several times already. As you prepare to hit the road, it's crucial to really get everything organized and accounted for.

As you pack, you'll find that there might be a few things that you don't quite have a spot for. This happens to every single person as they pack up for their maiden voyage. It is highly likely that you will overpack due to "The Unknown," which will leave you scrambling for space.

Many of us pack like we're fleeing quickly, but the good news about gearing up for your new life in a van is that you have time to be strategic and plan what you pack.

Clothing

When it comes to clothing, you're probably thinking you'll need a few day-time outfits, something comfortable to wear while driving, stuff to hike and do other outdoor activities in, and probably something civilized to wear if you decide to go out to a restaurant, museum, or other "citified" location.

It's important to note, that most clothing can do a lot of work in between washings. The jeans you wear while driving might be perfectly fine for touring a local art museum. The leggings you wear while hiking through a National Park might do the trick for driving long distances the next day.

That's not to say that clothing won't get soiled or damaged and need immediate laundry or replacement, but it's unlikely that you'll need to prepare with four pairs of pants per day. Instead, plan to hand wash anything that needs immediate attention (which you can handle in your dish tub — making the most out of everything!).

If you plan to do a lot of outdoor activities, you will want to make sure you pack plenty of clean, appropriate socks and the correct footwear. You might find yourself packing more pairs of shoes than pairs of jeans, depending on what your trip has in store for you. Hiking, running, canoeing, rock climbing or caving, and water sports all require different types of footwear, as well as storage options that can contain mud, dirt, water, and odor.

Additionally, you'll need to make sure you've got climate-related gear. Fleece jackets, water-proof windbreakers, swimsuits, and even sweaters or sweatshirts might be a great thing to pack. Just remember — you don't need to bring ALL of them.

If you're the type to overpack for a vacation, start by pulling everything you want to take with you out of the drawers and closets. Then reduce that by half. Then reduce by half again. Keep paring down until you have about seven to ten days of clothing options. You might want to check out the Capsule Wardrobe method and apply this to your overall wardrobe selection. Your goal is to carry less but to have more options.

You can always wash your clothes. You can always buy something on the road if a particular need arises. But once you're on the road, the only way to get rid of things you want to keep is to pack them up and ship them to someone who will store them for you!

Supplies

And then you've got all of your supplies. This can range from your break-down kit to your pots and pans, to your toiletries, and so on.

If you've got built-in cabinetry, that's going to solve a lot of problems. At the same time, remember that your van or skoolie is going to be in motion. That means braking, accelerating, hard turns, winding roads, bumps, and potholes. The objects in your cabinets will shift and move, which can make a mess, or leave a bump on your head in the case of overhead bins.

Many van dwellers like to create storage solutions that prevent things from moving around too much while the van is in motion. One way to do this is to group items in plastic bins. Bins with lids can be especially helpful when it comes to making sure vital supplies don't escape and roll around while you're driving. There are also rack-style shelving solutions that can be installed in cabinets that help keep things stable. Velcro, magnets, bungee-style cords, tie-downs, and more are all very helpful resources in keeping things in place during transit, too.

If you do use bins, it's a good idea to keep them all labeled or color-coded for easy access. Additionally, make sure certain items can be accessed inside or outside the van. It's unlikely that you'll want to open the rear door and stand in the pouring rain to find a can opener.

Anything you can do to make the contents of your van stable and accessible will go a long way toward extending the comfort and usability of your van's contents. For the most part, this will take practice. Things that seem to make sense before you hit the road might take a different shape once you get used to the overall flow of van living.

Chapter 4: Emergency Kit

When you think of an "Emergency Kit," the first thing that probably comes to mind is a first aid kit. A first aid kit is an absolute necessity, but the emergency kit includes so much more. After all, you're preparing for unplanned events in a home that's on wheels, powered by many moving mechanical parts.

When thinking about what to put in your emergency kit, first consider the relatively common incidents that might occur to a motor vehicle. For example, flat tires. If you're driving a large transit bus, you're not going to be able to just head over to the shoulder and pop the spare on. But for smaller vans, a spare tire, jack, and tire iron are a great idea. You might even bring a tire patch kit, in the event of minor issues that can be addressed shortly at a tire shop.

What about jumper cables or a battery jump kit? Many of the older vans don't include automatic headlights or even an annoying buzz or beep to let you know you've left your lights on. You don't want to be stuck in the middle of actual nowhere, with no cell phone signal and no battery power.

A fire extinguisher is a very important addition to any emergency kit. Depending on the size of your vehicle, you might want to bring a few along, for the inside of the vehicle and for the vehicle itself. While a fire is unlikely, it is possible. And if you're planning to brave the wilderness? You might not be within easy access of emergency services.

A tarp may seem unnecessary. After all, vans and buses have roofs, and they're pretty leak proof. The issue is the windows. Glass is prone to cracks and breakage, and having water streaming through the inside of your van is no one's idea of a good time. While a tarp and duct tape aren't a permanent fix, they will help take care of the issue while you create a plan. Tarps also make a pretty handy landing pad, tent base, canopy for loung-ing outside, "spare room," and more. If you're using an outdoor hanging shower, you can use the tarp as your "floor" so you don't have to stand in mud. The uses go on and on, making a pretty convincing argument for having a tarp on hand... just in case!

Battery-operated lighting is also a good idea. This can take the form of flashlights, small lanterns, and more. Don't rely on your cell phone flashlight as a light source. If you find yourself without power and need light for a lengthy period of time, using your phone flashlight will just drain the battery. Instead, save that battery, and use a device that doesn't have the ability to call for help! Make sure you pack spare batteries as well — don't assume that you'll be able to get more whenever you need them. Batteries take up very little room and are worth it to not find yourself in a dark and scary situation.

Solar flashlights and lanterns are also fine options — just make sure you let them see the sun during the day, so they're charged when you need them.

Depending on where you're going to spend your time, you might want an emergency water purification kit on hand. While you'll largely be able to plan ahead to manage your water supply, you might find yourself in a dry location with a leak. Being able to instantly replenish your water supply is a huge benefit, no matter where you are, or what type of adventure you're having. If you're relying on a fixed freshwater tank, make sure you have a backup plan. That can even mean having a few gallons of drinking water from the grocery store on hand — just make sure you've got them stashed away in a safe location, where they can't move around and possibly spring a leak while you're driving!

Having a spare gasoline can onboard can also be helpful, especially if you're going to be traveling through long stretches of uninhabited territory. The most important consideration for having gasoline onboard is storing it properly, so it doesn't tip and spill, become too hot or too cold, or accidentally release harmful fumes into the cabin. If you have children or pets with you, you'll want to be absolutely certain they can't accidentally come in contact with the gasoline directly, either.

If you've learned some of the basics of vehicle maintenance, you'll want to have a toolset onboard also. Generally speaking, this will include a hammer or mallet, and the right-sized wrenches for all of the pieces and parts within your vehicle. You might also want a screwdriver that fits the interior screws, just in case something works loose. First-time van dwellers are always a bit surprised at what things work loose when traveling consistently over bumpy roads! There's no need to take any tools that have no use in your vehicle, so make sure you pack wisely and organize well. A small toolbox or carrying case will save you tons of frustration when you're already upset about a breakdown.

Other helpful things to have onboard are items that have plenty of practical uses. Duct tape is almost always helpful for one reason or another. From temporarily taping the soles back onto your shoes, to holding a loose cabinet door down until you can fix it, to waterproofing a baseball cap, nearly every van dweller has some zany story involving duct tape coming to the rescue in a pinch. Make sure you invest in the truly waterproof, truly sticky stuff, too.

Multi-tools, such as Leatherman or Swiss Army Knives, will prove useful in a variety of situations, as well. You'll be thrilled to have one of these in your kit when you lose the nail clippers, need to cut something to size, try to open a bottle... the list goes on and on. A pocket-sized utensil with nearly infinite uses is always welcome in a van.

Matches or a long grill-style lighter can also be helpful. If you have a propane stove or burner that you'll be using, these will be a necessity, as well as if you plan on regularly building campfires. Even if you don't plan on needing to start a fire, you might find yourself in need of a heat and light resource if you lose your power source. Camping matches are a small easy-to-store investment that could really come in handy in a pinch.

In some cases, you'll want to pack several of these items. If, for example, you're a whole family on the road, you'll probably want several flashlights, which means stocking up on more batteries. If you're going to be gone for a significant amount of time, it can't hurt to have two rolls of duct tape — one in the cabin, and one on reserve with the vehicle maintenance equipment.

Now the tricky part — where do you put all of this stuff? With the exception of items that need special storage considerations, like gasoline and water, you might choose to put everything together in a tote or cabinet that is exclusively designated for your emergency kit. However, you might want to keep some of the smaller items in an easy-to-reach spot, like the glove box, or a small in-cabin kit that can be accessed quickly. After all, it makes no sense to have a flashlight if you have to fumble around in the dark in order to find it.

When it comes to emergency supplies, there's a fine line between "too prepared" and "possible catastrophe." Just like in a stationary home, it's impossible to prepare for every eventuality. It may seem even more challenging to think of all the dangers that might befall you on the road. In order to give yourself more peace of mind, do some research beforehand on the areas where you'll be traveling. What types of perils have other van dwellers encountered? Do other travelers have recommendations for supplies to have on hand? Knowing what others have experienced in that area can help give you some perspective on your own needs so you can plan ahead.

Chapter 5: Food

The topic of food has come up several times, and for good reason — we literally cannot live without it. In our stationary worlds, we pop into the grocery store whenever we need to and load up on fresh produce, meats, cheese, eggs, frozen foods, and so on. We bring them home, organize them in our full-sized refrigerators, freezers, and cabinets, and plan to use them before the expiration date. Sometimes we don't feel like cooking, so we head out to a restaurant or order delivery, and if we order too much food, we throw that in the refrigerator and reheat it in our microwaves the next day.

It is technically still possible to do all of that in a van or bus, as long as you've got the space, power, and equipment to do so. You may not have full-sized appliances and cabinets, but you can incorporate smaller, camper-style units that do the same job. This is a very good idea if you'll be traveling with children, or if you're making van living your permanent lifestyle.

For many Van Lifers, though, there is neither room nor practical need for appliances. In reality, none of the traditional kitchen appliances are required to live. An economical use of food products, a cold storage option, and the ability to heat food and water are really all it takes to keep yourself fed on the road.

As mentioned earlier, coolers are very helpful. The type of cooler you choose does have some bearing on your food options and usage, however. An ice-chest type cooler is typically very inexpensive, and melted ice can be recycled as bathwater or used for cleaning up certain non-food items (like the floor of the van, your muddy flip-flops, etc.). The downside to this is that your cooler will fill with water as the ice melts. Unless it is replenished regularly, that means that anything in the cooler can get water-logged, and anything that gets too warm has a chance of spoiling. But, if you practice extreme discipline in the use of your ice chest, there's no reason why this can't work.

Plug-in coolers can be very helpful, too. They are generally more expensive than ice chests, but you have the luxury of never worrying about the ice/water ratio. At the same time, you've got to have the power supply to keep it going. Most units require 12 volts of power, which isn't unreasonable. If you've got an older van with no power supply, however, you might be wary of leaving it plugged in overnight, as it might drain the battery. Some coolers will have the ability to keep their contents cooled if unplugged for short periods, and some will not. Food poisoning while on the road is even more un-comfortable than it is in a house or apartment, so don't tempt the fates when it comes to food safety. Make sure your food is stored at the appropriate temperature — if your cooler can't handle it, don't take the risk.

When it comes to storing produce, you have two main goals. The first is to not have it rolling around the cabin as you drive, and the second is to not attract insects or other wildlife that might be interested in sampling your meals. Generally speaking, the cooler is a fine place to keep your fruits and veggies, even if you wouldn't technically put a particular item there at home.

As for dry foods, the goals are the same as produce, only you won't necessarily want to stash everything in the cooler. Food-safe plastic storage tubs are a very good idea for things like rice and noodles and grains, as they keep the bugs out and all of the food in one place. Canned goods and other self-storing foods(like ramen noodle packets) only need to be stored in a way that they're secure and not rolling underfoot while you're trying to drive.

Snack foods and bread products are a different consideration on the road. At home, you might roll up the bag inside the cracker box, throw a chip-clip on a bag of crispy snacks, and just keep the bread shut with a twist-tie. On the road, you've got a greater exposure to insects, and living in an open-air type environment means things will go stale and grow mold more quickly. You've also got to consider curious wildlife, as well. Make sure you can tuck your snacks and bread products somewhere safe where they won't be shared without your permission.

If you're an avid camper or outdoor fan, you probably associate foods like peanut butter, trail mix, power bars, tuna, canned stew, and ramen with living outdoors. These are certainly staples of Van Life, as well, but you can diversify your diet. The key is making sure you use everything immediately, unless you have sufficient, reliable cold storage for leftovers.

When you go to the grocery store now, you might take advantage of sales, like 3 for $10 salad kits or "fill the freezer" meat deals. Without a ton of cold storage space, that's no longer going to make sense. Instead, you'll want to purchase only what you can eat or adequately store right now.

That's not to say you can't have salad or meat but that you'll want to look at portions realistically to avoid waste.

Canned and dried food is always a go-to when it comes to living in a situation where there's not a lot of space, time, or refrigeration, but these foods are often high in sodium and preservatives. Make sure you're making wise choices for your body, health, and lifestyle. Good nutrition is key to giving you stamina and helping you maintain your health while you're on the road. Make sure you're fueling your body in a way that's appropriate for you.

When planning meals, you can always take advantage of what resources you have to create back-to-back meals that will meet the requirements of multiple food groups. For example, if you purchase one salad kit, one can of beans, a bell pepper, two tomatoes, and one large chicken breast, you can have a protein-packed chicken/bean chili for dinner with a tasty side salad, then follow it up with a big salad topped with chicken for lunch the next day. Simply cook the chicken first, then cut it into two portions — the amount you'll add to tonight's chili and the bit that you'll slice up for lunch tomorrow. Make sure you put what you're not using right away into the cooler immediately. Throw the beans, a chopped tomato, and half the bell pepper into a pot with the chicken and your favorite seasonings for a tasty "road chili." Make yourself a small salad to enjoy, too, and make sure you seal up the rest and store it in the cooler. Tomorrow, you can use the other half of the bell pepper, the second tomato, the rest of the salad kit, and the leftover chicken to have a nutritious salad.

This is just one example of how being strategic with your food and resources can help you avoid "camp food burnout." There are plenty of recipe guides for low tech and outdoor living, and we've included some links in the **resources** at the end of this book. You might feel now like having a cooler and a propane camp stove will be incredibly limiting, but the reality is that you can eat almost exactly like you do at home — you just have to scale back and be more realistic about your food use. Before you start your maiden voyage, you might want to keep track of what you cook, what you eat, how many leftovers you have, and how quickly you eat those left-overs. This will give you a little more insight about your food volume usage, so you can be more adequately prepared once you get on the road.

Section 5: Where Are You Going to Go?

Your van is fully packed. You're ready to go. You're equipped with all sorts of new and exciting knowledge.

So where do you go?

For some people, there's a very obvious destination in mind. Perhaps you've spent your life pining for a visit to a particular landmark, park, or museum. Naturally, you'll want to head there immediately. But the beauty of van living is that there are no destinations — only the amazing journey. Once you've hit your ideal spot — then what? You might be feeling a bit lost.

Other people might not have a clear destination selected. They might have a few general ideas of things they'd like to see, but they haven't really figured out where to go or how to get there.

Then there's a third party, which borrows a little from the first group and the second group. These folks have a definite list of things they want to see but look forward to connecting the dots with adventure.

There's plenty of grey area in between these three options, as well. If you're worried about feeling constricted by requiring plans, you'll be glad to know that there's really no wrong way to do your Van Life. It is your practice, your lifestyle, and we're just here to tap you on the shoulder and give you practical advice and suggestions. If you're the sort of person who needs guidance or help getting started, that's also not wrong. You're allowed to be confused and overwhelmed.

Let's take a look at a few different strategies that are popular among road warriors. If you're feeling too decisive, this might help you open your mind to more possibilities. If you're feeling too free, this can help you start to reach out and explore a few solid "x" marks to put on your map for future destinations.

The "Keep Moving" Strategy

Have you ever heard the phrase "goes as the wind blows?" There are van dwellers who truly do this. If they wake up and feel like checking out the west coast, so be it. Maybe the mountains next week. How about a forest?

Having a home on wheels really does mean you can go where you want, when you want, but remember that fuel costs are a very real thing. If you have an unlimited budget, perhaps driving in perpetual circles and constantly being on the move isn't a bad thing. For those who need to be aware of every cent they spend, perhaps a little bit of planning can help temper that possible spending.

Navigation is a necessary evil, even if you just want to wander. While getting lost can be fun, it does lose its novelty when bad things happen, and you don't know where you are. It can also wind up feeling a little unnecessary and uninspiring over time.

Ultimately, the "Keep Moving" strategy can turn up some wonderful roadside surprises that you never expected to find. These lifetime experiences can never be forced, anticipated, or replaced. There is so much beauty in this world, and having the freedom to experience all the beauty you can is something many people can't even imagine.

This method does require a bit of careful compromise between wandering and respecting your budget, as well as any needs you might have for bathing, laundry, and stocking up on supplies. There needs to be a bit of conscious planning but never so much that you feel restricted.

Long-Term Living

Other people like to have the opportunity to really experience the culture of a location, even if it's just for a temporary time period.

While you might stake a claim on a particular camping spot, either within a designated camp park or out in the wilderness, that doesn't mean you can't leave and explore. As discussed earlier, some van dwellers take along a scooter or bicycle, so they can leave the confines of the van to wander — you're only limited by how far you're willing to stray from the van in one day.

Much like wandering, there are both pros and cons to this type of adventure. You might end up spending more in camping fees, due to your long-term stay, but you'll likely save on your fuel budget. Even if you do your local exploration in your van, it's likely that you'll be staying within a 20-mile radius.

Additionally, you'll be familiar with the area and some of the local options. You'll establish a place to purchase groceries, do your laundry, and replenish supplies. You might find some local entertainment options that you'd never expect to experience. Locals are a great source of knowledge, input, and recommendations that you won't find anywhere else, so it might be worth it to hang out at the local watering hole and find out when the county fair is or what local band is playing soon.

At the same time, you might find yourself feeling just a little too cozy. You might start to think that you've given up one home and just moved somewhere else. Always remember — you have the freedom to start the engine and throw it into gear anytime you want. Just figure out the next place to go, and get those actual wheels in motion!

Connecting the Dots
One fun method of travel is to turn the whole experience into a wild game of "connect the dots." You can pick a handful of things you'd really like to do while you're on the road, then mosey from point to point.

There are no restrictions on this method. You choose your timeframe and how you get from Point A to Point B. The only limits that exist are those that you create. For example, if you want to go to a concert in a specific city on a specific day, you'll need to make sure you make appropriate travel plans. Otherwise, you have the freedom to wander, without the lack of direction. In many ways, this is the best of both worlds!

Advice from the Road: Part 7

Our trip started as a fifty-page list of things we wanted to see, categorized by state. Yes. You read that right — fifty pages. There was no possible way we were going to be able to squeeze everything in, and we knew that, but still, it seemed like a good way to start.

Our first step was to pull out a huge map of the United States, including major freeways. This map was really huge — it took up our entire dining room table.

Next, we used little dot stickers to plot out some of the places we wanted to go, state by state. We put everything on there. In some states, it looked absolutely ridiculous. In other states, it was clear that we had a concentration of interest in a specific area.

The plans started to take shape from there. We knew we had a limited timeframe for our first trip (if you can call a year "limited"), so we had to create a way to see as much as possible without being too indirect.

We made a few rules to make sure we kept with our desire to explore: First, we would limit our use of major freeways and take as many back roads as possible. Second, any time we stopped, we'd check out what was going on in a five-mile radius and see what we needed to check out before we kept moving on.

We cheated a little on both of those rules. We broke the "five-mile rule" a lot, and there were a few times when we were so tired, we decided to take the fastest route instead of the scenic route to make sure we were driving safely. Still, I have absolutely no regrets about the number of things we were able to see, do, and try, and the diversity of those experiences.

Section 6: Staying Happy on the Road

We started this book by guiding you through the Van Life mindset, to see if you're prepared for this undertaking. After all, creating an entirely new lifestyle from scratch is no small task! At this point, you've got your vehicle. It's packed. You're confidently armed with a variety of literature, including repair manuals, replacement part specs, maps, pamphlets, recipes, and so on.

You probably feel pretty well prepared for anything that could happen, and you really should feel confident with all you have accomplished up to this point. Van Life is not for the weak of heart, and preparing for life on the road is a serious rite of passage.

Still, there's really nothing that can prepare you for the feeling you'll get, sitting behind that giant steering wheel, listening to your engine complain as it climbs its first winding mountain road with you.

And there's also nothing quite like the feeling of lying awake at night, on your van mattress, wishing for the thick memory foam bed you had at home, where you can fall asleep to your favorite Netflix series without worrying about burning up the power supply, in air conditioning that you can crank when it gets hot, with a shower and a toilet that require little to no maintenance in the very next room. You might just find yourself longing for a place that doesn't kind of faintly smell like shoes and laundry all the time. That's ok! You're entirely allowed to have these feelings.

In this section, we'll focus on how to keep the motivation and feelings of well-being continue even if life is starting to feel stale. While we can't cure your melancholy, we do want you to know that this is normal and happens to absolutely everyone.

Chapter 1: Avoiding Boredom

During particularly long hauls, you will likely experience boredom. Your first reaction to recognizing this boredom may be fear. You uprooted your entire life to live on the road, only to feel the same boredom you felt at home. What is wrong with you?

The answer? Nothing. You're allowed to feel stagnant, especially when you are.

The beauty of Van Life is that you can shake it up. Celebrate that you can go anywhere. If you start feeling like "all I do is drive, and I don't even like it," then go to a National Park. Hike the trails no one hikes. Or, if you're feeling lonely, hike the trails that everyone hikes. Meet new trail buddies. Let yourself be in awe of the natural beauty that surrounds you.

If, at any time, you feel like you see the same stuff every day, you need to find some hidden gems to get you out of the rut. Hop on the internet. Go into a diner or dive bar and talk to the older locals. In your life at home, you could break out of a rut by calling your friends and doing something predictable, like meeting up for coffee or a movie or drinks. On the road, if you're feeling the monotony, you need to go meet Sue, the World's Largest Cow (or whatever is "cool and unusual" in your vicinity). Do an online search for "cool and unusual things" and a location, and you'll turn up loads of things you've never even heard about!

Find out what's going on at the local college. What bands are playing? What kind of lectures or exhibitions can you find? If nothing comes to mind, just park at the end of a street, any street, walk until you don't want to keep going, then walk back to your van. You might wonder what that will accomplish. Well, what are five things you saw during your walk that were interesting?

Keep yourself in the mindset that you have control over your exploration. Though not every place you wander will feature jaw-dropping scenery, activities that make your heart race, or experiences that open your soul, there will be plenty of things that will be new to you. Embrace these.

You'll also want to keep your mind engaged while you're on the road, with activities you can enjoy within the confines of the van. There will be bad weather days. You will probably get sick or injured. Or, you just might not feel like leaving the van on a particular day. Make sure you have plenty of stuff that will keep you engaged and entertained.

A few examples include:

- Audiobooks, music, and podcasts. You don't have to stop learning and growing, just because you're no longer a part of a wall-to-wall, brick-and-mortar society! Use this opportunity to expand your horizons. Choose audiobooks that teach you about totally new topics. Listen to performers you've only heard about from your friends. Check out podcasts that will challenge your thoughts and endear you to the human experience.
- Activity books. This may seem like it's geared to kids, but adults can gain a lot from coloring, doing logic puzzles, crosswords, sudoku, or even by trying to find Waldo! When you stare at the road for hours at a time, your mind craves something different, so put your creativity and problem-solving skills to the test with some harmless activities that won't require a lot of space or supplies.
- Blogging. Though a brief glimpse through the **resources section** may make it sound like the internet is already saturated with Van Life blogs, there's always room for your experience. You can start a blog for free and use it to share your pictures and thoughts with friends and family. You might also start a variety of social media platforms specifically for your voyage. If sharing these thoughts with the whole world isn't your style, old fashioned pen-and-paper journals are always an option.

Lastly, try to take a deep breath and remember to enjoy the moment. It is very easy for depression and anxiety to creep up on you when you're on the road, especially if you're alone. As you drive, you have lots of time to stop and reflect on negative thoughts. It's easier said than done, but don't let your mind trick you like that.

Come up with a mantra that reaffirms your abilities. You have made it this far. You have created a new lifestyle for yourself. You are doing just fine. Today is always an adventure, and you have opportunities on the road that many people will never take advantage of. Remind yourself to love what you're doing. Cherish every detail, every new experience, every little thing you've never seen before.

This is your dream, and you are making it come true.

Chapter 2: Homesickness/Loneliness

Being on the road can feel very lonely sometimes. Most of us are used to living a more sedentary lifestyle or one where we can just pick up the phone and text or call our friends. You and your buddies probably get together now and then to catch up, have dinner, watch movies, and just generally hang out. It's different when you're on the road.

You can still have friends over to your van, of course, but now you have to meet new people. You'll probably visit friends and family that you don't usually get to see while you're traveling, but all the people you see every day will be exactly where you left them.

While this concept might make you feel very sad, that's not entirely bad news. They're exactly where you left them. You can go visit them. Some people feel that, since they're devoted to Van Life now, they can't go home. It's ok to go home.

There is going to come a time when both your body and soul will long for the comforts and conveniences of home. If you have the desire to go back to the place where you started your journey, go for it! Stay with friends or family back in your hometown. Go to your regular haunts. Everyone will want to hear stories, so share them! Soon, your heart will long for the road again, and off you'll go, spiritually refreshed from your visit.

You might also try planting for a bit wherever you are on the road. Find a long-term parking solution, and let yourself have a routine for a few days. Sometimes the brain and body need a sense of regularity and stability to help you put everything into perspective.

Additionally, keep your finger on the pulse of the van community. There are plenty of meetups scheduled throughout the year, even around the world. You might start conversing with your new best friends via the forums, blogs, and social media sites dedicated to those living the Van Life. Becoming a part of a community can help you with those feelings of longing and belonging.

Advice from the Road: Part 8
The first time you miss an important family event, it will break your heart. You'll see the pictures online — maybe your whole family enjoying cake together — and you'll wish you were there. You'll be able to feel all the hugs, hear the laughter, smell the over-cooked casserole, and your heart will cry out.

The first event I missed was my niece's birthday party. It was a small shindig, and really not a big deal, but when I saw the pictures of her opening her gifts, beaming at the camera, surrounded by torn wrapping paper and the bounty of her party, I cried. I wanted to be there. But it wasn't practical to be there and here, 800 miles away in the middle of the mountains.

Sometimes, you'll feel like you've done something selfish. People will try to tell you that, too. But the reality is that we all choose the lifestyle that's best for us.

You can choose to come home for the holidays, the birthdays, the anniversaries, the bachelorette parties, and so on. But the realities of time and space mean that you can't be in two places at once. You can't summit Angel's Landing and be in Florida by dinner time.

Remember that you can make room for everything and anything that you value, but you don't have to make room for everything and anything that's suggested to you. You can always go back. You can always come back. Don't let yourself feel rushed or pushed.

One tool that I began to value from the road was phone calls. It's so easy to get away with texting conversations, but when you're on the road, hearing someone's voice can be very soothing. It's also likely that there's someone who wants to hear from you, too. When you have a fully-charged battery and service, reach out — make a call. Talk. It'll do your soul some good.

Chapter 3: Housekeeping

Housekeeping might not be the most enjoyable use of time, but it's extremely necessary. If you're the type who has a "junk drawer," a "mail folder," or "a laundry chair". You might find Van Life challenging at first.

In a van, any mess you make is proportionately larger than it would be in a house or apartment. If you leave a pair of shoes on the floor of your bedroom, you can probably maneuver around them pretty easily. If you leave your shoes on the floor of your van, you will trip over them, and you will get mad at yourself for leaving them where you could trip over them.

Living in close quarters requires a new level of hygiene, which can be especially tricky when you don't have the ability to give yourself hour-long exfoliating showers every day. Keeping the stinky things stored, as we mentioned earlier, is a great way to prevent a long-term, permanent reek, but you'll still need to wash everything regularly. That includes your-self, your laundry, your bed linens, any rugs you might have, your dishes, and your commode, just to name a few. Make sure you dispose of spoiled food immediately. If you are practicing recycling on the road, make sure your empties are rinsed.

Not only do these practices cut down on bad smells, but they also cut down on bugs and critters. Wildlife is a very real part of Van Life and can include everything from the innocuous visits of birds, squirrels, and chipmunks, to the possibly dangerous curiosity of bears. You'll definitely want to avoid the headache of an ant infestation, but there's no reason to tempt a hungry grizzly!

To avoid all of this, make sure you sweep your abode on wheels regularly. Clean up any spills immediately. Get rid of trash as frequently as you can. Do your part to keep things as clean as possible.

Not only does this practice have sanitary implications, but it can also make you feel better about your dwelling. Some people feel a sense of purpose and pride when they mow their lawn or scrub their floors in a stationary home. Doing something as simple as washing all of the mud from your latest off-road excursion can remind you that you love your new home and your new life, and you wouldn't have it any other way!

In Conclusion

Is Van Life for everyone? No. The truth is that most people won't even consider, think about, or be able to fathom the idea of living in a small, mobile space. The idea of not knowing where you're going to sleep tonight, or heating up beans over a propane burner in the dark, or going to the bathroom outside at midnight might sound like an absolute nightmare to some people.

But there is a special breed of people. There are some who hear or read phrases like this, and their hearts beat a little faster and a little harder. The ideas of "opportunities" and "unknowns" sound more welcoming than fearsome. They look at the walls around them and feel like they're being crushed by stability. These are the people who are born Van Lifers.

Are you one of them? Only you can tell for sure. If there is one thing we hope you've learned from this book, it's that you can't do Van Life the wrong way. Beyond that, building your own Van Life is a process and not one that comes quickly or easily.

Can you find "any old" van, start the engine, and take off? Sure! There are some people who are naturally adaptive. But for those of us who are taking off from what feels like a very sheltered spot, there can be lots of planning and attention to details in order to feel more secure about this huge decision.

If there's one piece of advice all van dwellers should know, it's "Don't panic when things go wrong — they just will." The first time things go topsy-turvy, it will be terrifying. There will be setbacks. You will revisit the drawing board many times. The good news is that, even when things go upside down, they tend to put themselves right sideup again, as long as you don't panic.

Remember also that this isn't a competition. Just because someone on social media does it differently, doesn't mean you've failed. If you catch a cold and spend two days in a hotel recovering, that doesn't mean you're inadequate. It means you did the best thing you could for yourself in that situation. If you choose to start the day with your favorite chain restaurant doughnut and coffee, don't feel like your experience is any less authentic than the bloggers who figure out how to make overnight oats in a tin coffee mug. Just make sure you budget for the expense and get on with your best Van Life.

In short, be sure to enjoy every step of the journey. You are doing something many people dream of, but very few people get to experience.

This is the beginning of your new life.

Section 7: Helpful Resources for Future Van Dwellers

The following links lead to online blogs, reference materials, and websites that can help you with every step of the process of converting to Van Life. The views and ideas expressed in each of these links belong solely to the person writing it, so please don't consider their inclusion an endorsement or partnership. We simply wanted to get you started on the quest for more information.

Remember, there is no "wrong" way to do Van Life. There are only ways that work better for your lifestyle and things that don't work for you. It's a very personal experience that often requires a lot of trial and error.

Still, sometimes it helps to read the experiences of those who have tried it, are doing it, or are in the same position as you are when it comes to trying something very, very different.

Feel free to check out some of these links to draw inspiration, and continue your quest for more information!

The Van Life State of Mind:
As noted, you've got to be in the right headspace to really enjoy the wild ride.

http://www.alwaystheroad.com/blog/2017/3/24/is-van-life-for-you-how-to-know-if-its-right-for-you

Parking Options, Camping Options, and Sleep Spots
Tracking down a spot where you can catch up on some rest or spend the night can be challenging, especially when you're on a tight budget. Here are some resources to help you find a safe, practical place to rest.

https://www.campendium.com/camping/vanlife/
http://thevanual.com/sleeping-and-safety/

https://www.cheaprvliving.com/stealth-city-parking/bobs-12-command-ments-for-stealth-parking-in-the-city/
https://divineontheroad.com/overnight-parking/
https://kombilife.com/van-life-free-camping/
https://www.classicvans.com/
https://www.youtube.com/watch?v=oqPiP2JYVNc
https://www.nps.gov/index.htm

Choosing a Van

If the topic of vans as a vehicle is new to you, you'll definitely want to do additional research before starting the shopping process. Here are a few sites that will help you learn more about the types of vans and buses, as well as a variety of opinions to help guide you through the pros and cons of every option out there.

https://www.curbed.com/2018/1/31/16951486/best-van-conversion-rv-camper-vanlife
https://vanclan.co/best-van-to-live-in/
https://gnomadhome.com/why-choose-conversion-van-for-vanlife/
https://gearmoose.com/van-life-best-camper-vans/
https://weretherussos.com/van-chassis-camper-van-conversion/

Classic Van Lifers

As mentioned, Classic vans have a following of their own. Here are some links to resources for people who are living the "old school" way, with vans from earlier eras. Check out their thoughts, experiences, and words of advice.

https://bearfoottheory.com/category/van-life/
https://blog.feedspot.com/van_life_blogs/
https://vanclan.co/vanlife-blogs/

Skoolies

For those who are interested in larger format on-the-road living, buses are the way to go. The conversion, rehab, remodel, and updating of these vehicles could be a book on their own, so we've included a few links to folks who have gone through the process. Their insights, advice, trials, and tribulations can be helpful as you adjust to the learning curve of a great big diesel vehicle!

https://gearjunkie.com/school-bus-rv-camper-conversion-remodel
https://www.curbed.com/2019/3/6/18246221/camper-conversion-skoo-lie-vanlife-tiny-house
https://www.buslifeadventure.com/index.php/blog/16-blog/198-bus-life-vs-van-life-as-seen-through-the-eyes-of-a-van-dweller

The Cost of Van Living
While we've included some details about how to calculate your van shopping budget, your remodeling budget, your road budget, your overall experience budget and more, we can't predict all of the expenses that might go into your individual experience. Check out these resources for more inspiration.

https://www.moneyunder30.com/van-living
https://www.parkedinparadise.com/van-life-cost/
https://mymoneywizard.com/living-in-a-van/
https://www.explorist.life/how-much-does-van-life-cost/
https://faroutride.com/vanlife-actual-cost/

Generating Revenue on the Road
Again, we all need to follow our own path when it comes to careers, so only try this at home if you think you can make it work with your own skills, talents, and preferences. If you're feeling hesitant about trying to make a career work on the road, here are some thoughts, ideas, and words of wisdom from those who have made it happen.
https://www.thewaywardhome.com/make-money-living-on-the-road/
http://www.alwaystheroad.com/blog/2017/9/18/the-ultimate-van-life-

question-answered-how-we-make-money-on-the-road

https://projectvanlife.com/van-life-money-tips/

https://vansage.com/remote-jobs-for-van-life/

https://outboundliving.com/working-making-money/

https://vacayvans.com/how-to-make-money-working-remotely-living-vanlife/

https://wandrlymagazine.com/article/make-money-in-a-van/

On the Topic of Food

Everyone has different tastes, so we tried to round up a bunch of links that cover food storage, food preparation, and on-the-road recipes that many people can relate to. The food suggestions we mentioned within the chapter aren't inclusive of all diets and preferences, so we wanted to help get the creative cooking ideas flowing with a handful of resources.

https://www.climbonmaps.com/cold-food-storage.html

https://authenticavl.com/van-life/how-to-keep-your-food-fresh/

https://vanclan.co/vanlife-recipes/

https://mpora.com/camping/12-super-simple-meals-for-when-youre-living-in-a-van/

https://www.vancognito.com/van-life-cooking/

https://www.allrecipes.com/article/three-ways-to-conquer-camper-van-cooking-vanlife/

https://vansage.com/easy-campsite-recipes/

https://theplaidzebra.com/these-5-cheap-and-easy-meal-ideas-will-give-you-the-freedom-to-take-life-on-the-road/

https://simplyvanlife.com/non-perishable-foods-for-van-life/

https://www.parkedinparadise.com/storage-organization/

http://www.nomadswithavan.com/van-friendly-foods/

https://www.youtube.com/watch?v=1zTzaeOo8_w

For Kristine Hudson and her husband Brad, the adventure never ends! If you enjoyed reading Ms. Hudson's insights on preparing for a life on the road in "How to Live the Dream: Things Every Van Lifer Needs to Know," you'll love catching up with her on her new Facebook page. For ladies who are curious about the daily ins and outs of being a Boss Lady after reading "How to Choose the Ultimate Side-Hustle: Making Money and Being Your Own Boss," Ms. Hudson shares her regular experiences with keeping herself organized while maintaining her writing and editing career.

It may seem that waking up every day in a new place and having a successful, satisfying career may be mutually exclusive. "Like" and "Follow" Kristine Hudson on Facebook to see her in action... and to catch a glimpse of her sometimes hectic, but always compelling, life on the road!

Kristine Hudson's Van Life: **https://www.facebook.com/eternalvantrip/**

also by Kristine Hudson

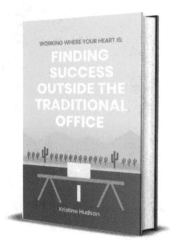

How to Choose the Ultimate Side-hustle

mybook.to/side-hustle

Finding Success Outside The Traditional Office

mybook.to/workfromanywhere

CPSIA information can be obtained
at www.ICGtesting.com
Printed in the USA
LVHW021317161121
703475LV00004B/265